HOW ABRAHAM LINCOLN FOUGHT THE CIVIL WAR

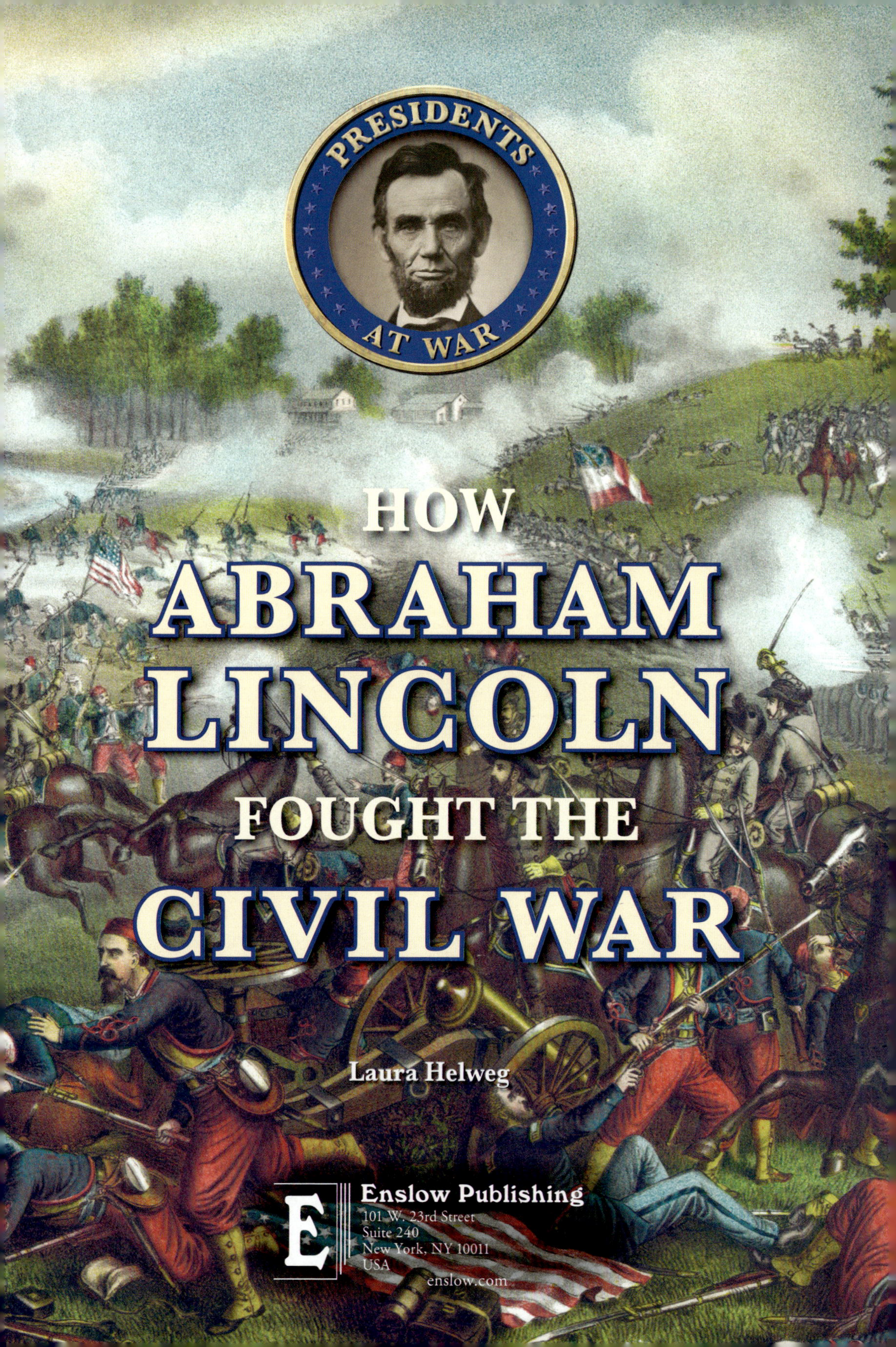

HOW ABRAHAM LINCOLN FOUGHT THE CIVIL WAR

Laura Helweg

Enslow Publishing
101 W. 23rd Street
Suite 240
New York, NY 10011
USA
enslow.com

Published in 2018 by Enslow Publishing, LLC.
101 W. 23rd Street, Suite 240, New York, NY 10011

Library of Congress Cataloging-in-Publication Data

Names: Helweg, Laura, author.
Title: How Abraham Lincoln fought the Civil War / Laura Helweg.
Description: New York : Enslow Publishing, 2018. | Series: Presidents at war | Includes bibliographical references and index. | Audience: Grades 7–12.
Identifiers: LCCN 2017003127 | ISBN 9780766085251 (library-bound)
Subjects: LCSH: Lincoln, Abraham, 1809-1865—Military leadership—Juvenile literature. | CYAC: United States—History—Civil War, 1861–1865—Juvenile literature.
Classification: LCC E457 .H45 2017 | DDC 973.7092 [B] —dc23
LC record available at https://lccn.loc.gov/2017003127

Printed in the United States of America

To Our Readers: We have done our best to make sure all website addresses in this book were active and appropriate when we went to press. However, the author and the publisher have no control over and assume no liability for the material available on those websites or on any websites they may link to. Any comments or suggestions can be sent by email to customerservice@enslow.com.

Photo Credits: Cover, pp. 1, 3, 7, 11, 23, 33, 45, 56, 62, 67, 80, 92, 104, 107 Library of Congress Prints and Photographs Division; p. 8 Kean Collection/Archive Photos/Getty Images; p. 10 Universal History Archive/Universal Images Group/Getty Images; p. 12 John Parrot/Stocktrek Images/Getty Images; p. 14 North Wind Picture Archives/Alamy Stock Photo; pp. 21, 34, 71, 82, 105 Buyenlarge/Archive Photos/Getty Images; pp. 26, 48 Corbis Historical/Getty Images; pp. 28, 43, 51, 84 National Archives; p. 36 NH 50954 courtesy of the Naval History and Heritage Command; p. 59 PF - (usna)/Alamy Stock Photo; p. 65 Fine Art/Corbis Historical/Getty Images; p. 69 G Seeger/Shutterstock.com; p. 75 MPI/Archive Photos/Getty Images; p. 78 Library of Congress Geography and Map Division; p. 93 The Protected Art Archive/Alamy Stock Photo; p. 96 GraphicaArtis/Archive Photos/Getty Images; p. 99 Archive Photos/Getty Images; pp. 109–115 (background) Everett Historical/Shutterstock.com.

CONTENTS

INTRODUCTION

> **"I do solemnly swear that I will faithfully execute the office of President of the United States, and will to the best of my ability, preserve, protect and defend the Constitution of the United States."**[1]

Abraham Lincoln was the sixteenth man to utter this presidential oath. Yet the responsibility of preserving, protecting, and defending the constitution had never before seemed such a herculean feat. By Lincoln's Inauguration Day, March 4, 1861, seven states had severed their bond with the United States and its founding document. They called their new country the Confederate States of America. Lincoln called it "the pretended authority" and refused to acknowledge it as a legal entity.[2] In fact, Lincoln believed that allowing disunion would violate his oath.

In his inaugural speech, Lincoln attempted to avert disaster. First, he reassured the South. Southerners believed Lincoln posed a threat to their slavery-dependent two days which had elapsed since its adjournment hither from Columbia, had been deliberating in secret session. A little after midday of December 20th, the streets of Charleston were filled with the following placards, giving the public the first notice of its action:

CHARLESTON MERCURY

EXTRA:

Passed unanimously at 1.15 o'clock, P. M., December 20th, 1860.

AN ORDINANCE

To dissolve the Union between the State of South Carolina and other States united with her under the compact entitled "The Constitution of the United States of America."

We, the People of the State of South Carolina, in Convention assembled, do declare and ordain, and it is hereby declared and ordained,

That the Ordinance adopted by us in Convention, on the twenty-third day of May, in the year of our Lord one thousand seven hundred and eighty-eight, whereby the Constitution of the United States of America was ratified, and also, all Acts and parts of Acts of the General Assembly of this State, ratifying amendments of the said Constitution, are hereby repealed; and that the union now subsisting between South Carolina and other States, under the name of "The United States of America," is hereby dissolved.

THE

UNION

IS

DISSOLVED!

ATTORNEY-GENERAL JEREMIAH S. BLACK.
(FROM A PHOTOGRAPH BY BRADY.)

The usual jubilations immediately followed, —ringing of bells, salutes of cannon, and the noise and display of street parades. The convention resolved to celebrate the event further by a public ceremonial to which it invited the governor, the legislature, and other dignitaries; and both branches of the legislature also sent a committee to Caleb Cushing to give him an official invitation to attend. At half-past 6 that evening the members of the convention marched in procession to Institute Hall, where the public signing of the ordinance of secession was performed with appropriate solemnities, and at its close the President announced: "The ordinance of secession has been signed and ratified, and I proclaim the State of South Carolina an Independent Commonwealth."

The city and the State joined in general exultation as if a great work had been accomplished, as if the efforts of a generation had been crowned with fulfillment, and nothing remained but to rest and enjoy the ripened fruit of independence. There seemed to be no dream, amid all this rejoicing, that nothing definite had as yet been effected; that the reckless day's act was but the prelude to the most terrible tragedy of the age, the unchaining of a storm which should shake the continent with terror and devastation, leaving every Southern State a wreck, and sweeping from the face of the earth the institution in whose behalf the fatal work was done.

The secession ordinance having been passed, signed, and proclaimed, the convention busied itself for the next few days in making up a public statement of its reasons for the anomalous procedure. The discussion showed a wide divergence of opinion as to the causes which had produced the act. One ascribed it to the election of Lincoln, another to the failure of the Northern States to execute the fugitive-slave law, a third to the antislavery sentiment of the free States, a fourth to the tariff, a fifth to unconstitutional appropriations by Congress, and so on. On the 24th of December the convention adopted a "Declaration of Causes," and an "Address to the Slaveholding States," the two papers together em-

A South Carolina newspaper announces the state's exit from the United States on December 20, 1860.

culture and economy despite his pledge, repeated that day on Pennsylvania Avenue, that "I have no purpose, directly or indirectly, to interfere with the institution of slavery in the States where it exists. I believe I have no lawful right to do so, and I have no inclination to do so."[3] Next, Lincoln appealed to logic with a courtroom argument against the legality of secession: "I hold that in contemplation of universal law and of the Constitution the Union of these States is perpetual."[4] In closing, Lincoln pleaded with the South. Sounding as if he were speaking to a beloved but wayward child, Lincoln announced:

> In your hands, my dissatisfied fellow-countrymen, and not in mine, is the momentous issue of civil war. The Government will not assail you. You can have no conflict without being yourselves the aggressors … We are not enemies, but friends. We must not be enemies.[5]

Lincoln was not prepared to be a war president. In addition to a nearly blank résumé in federal government, his only military experience was three months in the Illinois militia. Even so, Lincoln's uneventful time in the Black Hawk War sparked his interest in politics and hinted at his leadership skills. Remembering that the company had elected Lincoln captain, one friend later noted, "His heart & head were large & Comprehensive enough to Command a Company—regiment or other Core of men under any Circumstances."[6]

Instead of drawing on education or experience, Lincoln learned to command on the job. His military advisers tutored him on attacking fortified positions, moving troops and supplies, and battlefield ethics. Yet being outside of

A crowd gathered to hear Lincoln's first inaugural address. Lincoln directed most of the speech at his opponents, but the secessionists disregarded his eloquent pleas for peace.

military tradition also made Lincoln open to unconventional ideas. Embracing new inventions, enlisting black soldiers, and announcing a blockade of Southern ports with only a skeleton navy all earned Lincoln doubt and derision but eventually bore fruit that energized the nation toward victory.

Lincoln's career as commander in chief demonstrates a remarkable trajectory. In four years, he developed from a little-known and untried lawyer into the man who saved a nation from itself. As Vice President Hannibal Hamlin later reflected, "No man ever grew in the executive chair in his lifetime as Lincoln did."

"AND THE WAR CAME"[1]

Lincoln had to hit the ground running. His predecessor had spent the past four months avoiding the problem, and the rebellion now faced Lincoln fully formed. In the first hours of his first day as president, Lincoln received reports about an urgent situation in the seceded state of South Carolina.

> **"I am exceedingly anxious that the Union, the Constitution, and the liberties of the people shall be perpetuated in accordance with the original idea for which that struggle was made."**[2]
>
> —*Lincoln to the New Jersey legislature, February 1861*

Crisis in South Carolina

Fort Sumter, rising from an island in Charleston Harbor, had not received supplies since late 1860, when South Carolina declared its independence. The federal fort kept

Lincoln's cabinet frequently gathered in Lincoln's office. As they grappled with the Fort Sumter crisis in March 1861, Lieutenant General Winfield Scott often joined the sessions.

the stars and stripes flying but would have to surrender to the surrounding Confederate army if more rations and supplies didn't arrive soon. If Lincoln let the Southerners have the fort, he would be violating his duty as protector of the nation. Yet if he sent provisions and fresh soldiers, the Southerners might forcibly resist. The crisis at Fort Sumter presented a forked road: surrender to the secessionists or instigate a civil war.

Lincoln attempted to beat a path down the middle. He would send ships to Fort Sumter with food and nonmilitary supplies only. He notified South Carolina's governor that he would not send reinforcements unless the delivery met violence. Lincoln's warning gave Governor Francis Pickens an equally burdensome decision. Pickens either had to allow the federal government to hold the fort, or he had to initiate a war. For both leaders, acquiescence was unthinkable. In the predawn hours of April 12, the very day supplies were to arrive, Confederate cannons opened fire on Fort Sumter. The Civil War had begun.

With the curse of war, the shots at Fort Sumter also brought Lincoln the blessing of a determined public. Prior to the assault, Northerners wavered on whether to allow the South to leave. Now the public shouted in one voice for war. When Lincoln called for seventy-five thousand militiamen a few days later, the states overfilled their quotas. Ohio's governor, whose state filled twenty regiments instead of the required thirteen, summarized the mood: "The lion in us is thoroughly roused."[3]

Unfortunately, Fort Sumter also unified the South. Following the face-off, four more states seceded. They were Tennessee, Arkansas, North Carolina, and Virginia, which lay just across the Potomac River from Washington, DC. Lincoln could now view rebel territory from his office window.

Keeping "On Foot"

Yet Lincoln had few troops to protect the capital or the rest of the nation. The peacetime military had only seventeen thousand regular soldiers, who were spread over the western territories. Complicating the matter, one-third of the army's officers were Southern born. In the first days of war, 286 army and 322 navy officers resigned to join the Confederacy. The military also lacked the machinery of

This map shows the areas that were free vs. those that allowed slavery.

war. In March, Secretary of the Navy Gideon Welles could only find twelve ships ready to sail. Half of those were lost in April when the panicked commander of the Gosport Navy Yard in Norfolk, Virginia, destroyed the ships there to keep them from the approaching Confederates.

Complicating matters, the new legislature was not scheduled to meet until December 1861. Therefore, Congress—the government body with constitutional war powers—was not in session when the Civil War started. Yet Lincoln could not wait. One week after Fort Sumter, he ordered a blockade of Southern ports. In May, he requested regular soldiers who would serve for three years, despite the constitution's limits on presidential orders for troops.

Lincoln's Contrary Cabinet

Most presidents fill their cabinet with supporters. Lincoln, on the other hand, appointed rivals and critics as his advisers. He set aside personal feelings and past grievances to compile a cabinet that would shore up support from all sections of the population. Each appointment strengthened Lincoln's political position in the disintegrating nation.

William Seward, Secretary of State: A New York lawyer and politician, Seward was the front-runner for the Republican nomination until Lincoln overtook him. Seward's wife, Frances, ran an Underground Railroad stop at their home in Auburn, and Seward held the respect of abolitionists. As secretary of state, one of Seward's main duties was keeping foreign powers uninvolved in the war.

Simon Cameron, Secretary of War: Cameron was a political boss and senator from Pennsylvania who also contended for the Republican nomination. Because of Cameron's inefficiency and corruption, Lincoln replaced him with Edwin Stanton in January 1862.

Edward Bates, Attorney General: Another Republican presidential hopeful, the St. Louis lawyer belonged to the Whig Party, from which the Republicans had recently split. Lincoln hoped the Missourian's appointment would appease the slaveholding border states still in the Union. Bates's family exemplified the Civil War rift: one son fought for the Confederacy, another for the Union.

(continued on the next page)

(continued from the previous page)

Montgomery Blair, Postmaster General: The appointment of an idealistic abolitionist from Maryland curried favor with both antislavery groups and citizens loyal to the slaveholding state bordering the capital. Blair also brought military experience to the group; he was a former army officer and graduate of the US Military Academy at West Point.

Gideon Welles, Secretary of the Navy: A newspaper publisher from Connecticut, Welles's only naval experience was as the official in charge of feeding and clothing sailors. Lincoln selected Welles primarily for his New England address, but the spirited former Democrat proved to be an adept manager and oversaw the rapid expansion of the navy.

Caleb Smith, Secretary of the Interior: Smith was a congressman and railroad businessman. During the 1860 Republican convention, he seconded Lincoln's nomination and helped deliver the majority of Indiana's voters to the Lincoln ballot. Lincoln rewarded him with an appointment. Smith was a mediocre administrator and resigned in January 1863.

Salmon Chase, Secretary of the Treasury: Chase had also opposed Lincoln for the Republican nomination. The antislavery former senator and governor of Ohio was responsible for the growing burden of financing the war. However, Chase's desire for the presidency remained unsatisfied, and Lincoln fired him after Chase declared his candidacy for the 1864 election.

Lincoln also called Congress to session early. When the lawmakers arrived in July, he explained his actions: "Of all that which a President might constitutionally and justifiably do in such a case, everything was forborne without which it was believed possible to keep the Government on foot."[4] Congress agreed. It retroactively approved "all the extraordinary acts, proclamations, and orders" of the president.[5]

> **"The President shall be Commander in Chief of the Army and Navy of the United States."**
>
> —*US Constitution, Article II, Section 2*

The Border State Balance

Many of Lincoln's early actions focused on keeping the remaining slave states in the Union. In the second wave of secession following Fort Sumter, Kentucky, Missouri, Maryland, and Delaware did not follow their Southern brethren into the Confederacy. Lincoln believed the nation's survival depended largely on these states' continued loyalty. In addition to reiterating that he would leave slavery alone, Lincoln addressed unrest in each state in the way that would best cement that state's bond to the Union. Delaware caused few problems, but Kentucky, Missouri, and Maryland frequently demanded Lincoln's attention.

Maryland

Maryland's geography made the state particularly precarious. Maryland partially encircled Washington, DC, with seceded Virginia completing the capital city's border.

If Maryland joined the rebellion, the Union government would be surrounded by the enemy.

Yet pro-South and anti-Lincoln sentiments erupted in Maryland. On April 19, Baltimore rioters opposed troops traveling through the city to Washington. The mob pelted the soldiers with bricks and stones; then, someone in the crowd fired. The soldiers defended themselves as they continued toward the capital. By the end of the day, four soldiers and twelve civilians lay dead. Three days after the riot, Union general Benjamin Butler occupied Baltimore to prevent further violence. His forces also seized Maryland's capital, Annapolis.

Then in May, a Maryland legislator was arrested for harassing Union troops. To keep such dissidents from encouraging insurrection, Lincoln suspended the right to be imprisoned only if charged with a crime, known as habeas corpus, in the state. In September, Lincoln had government officials arrested and held without trial to prevent a vote about secession. Federal troops occupied Maryland for the remainder of the war.

Many considered these actions illegal; to Lincoln they were indispensable to maintaining the Union. Throughout the war, he would sacrifice some rights to uphold his chief constitutional responsibility.

Missouri

Missouri had been causing trouble even before Lincoln's election. Pro-slavery Missourians had been in a bloody border war with antislavery Kansans since 1854. Although Missouri's legislature voted against secession, most Missouri residents sided with the Confederacy. The pro-South governor even tried to use the state militia to occupy the state for the South. Federal troops defeated the governor's attack on a St. Louis military arsenal, but Confederate troops and sympathizers occupied swaths of Missouri through 1864.

Kentucky

Kentucky also had a majority of pro-South residents. However, instead of voting to leave or remain in the Union, the legislature declared Kentucky's neutrality—it would not join the Confederacy, but it would also not fight for the Union. Lincoln was disappointed by the lack of loyalty but decided to respect his birth state's decision and kept troops out of Kentucky. That is, he did until Confederate general Leonidas Polk invaded and occupied the city of Columbus.

Polk's move tipped Kentucky into Union lines. The governor invited Union troops in to oppose the Confederates, and General Ulysses S. Grant peacefully occupied Paducah, on the mouth of the Tennessee River, and Southland on the Cumberland River. Both waterways would ferry Union supplies throughout the war.

West Virginia

Although Virginia seceded after the Fort Sumter crisis, the western portion of the state was pro-Union. In fact, the counties west of the Appalachian Mountains themselves seceded from the rest of the state, and Lincoln sent General George McClellan to protect the inhabitants. In June and July, McClellan won several battles and secured the region. The state of West Virginia officially joined the United States in 1863.

Establishing a Strategy

As the summer heat of 1861 settled in, the two armies enlisted soldiers, piled up supplies, and drilled battle formations. Meanwhile, Lincoln and his advisers discussed strategy.

The Anaconda Plan

When the Civil War began, General Winfield Scott was the highest-ranking army officer and the White House's chief adviser on military matters. Scott, an inch taller than the president and twice as broad, had studied at the West Point academy and had commanded for half a century. When he spoke, others listened.

Scott adhered to the era's attitude toward war: gentlemen fought organized battles with as little violence as possible. Scott proposed attacking the Confederacy, not by invading the land, but by strangling the economy. The navy would block Southern ports on the Atlantic Ocean, the Gulf of Mexico, and the Mississippi River, cutting off the Confederacy's trade. Next, soldiers would attack strategic points from these navy-held positions. The Union would slowly strangle the South; then it would strike. Critics decried the delayed action and called it the Anaconda Plan.

"Forward to Richmond!"

This choke hold is exactly what Lincoln intended with the blockade. However, Lincoln wanted the anaconda approach immediately combined with inland efforts. Besides, the navy currently had only a handful of ships; Lincoln hoped the war wouldn't last long enough for a true blockade to form. He believed that one decisive battle would convince

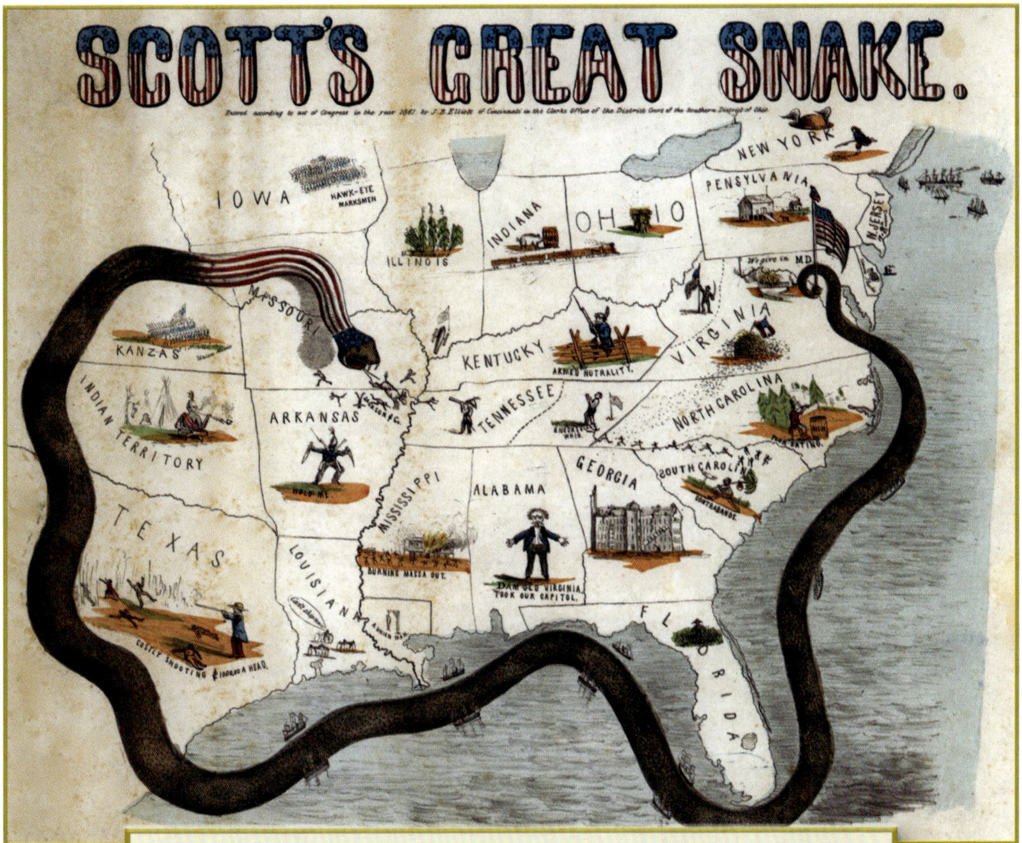

This cartoon scoffs at General Scott's plan to weaken the enemy's economy before full-scale combat. Scott's opponents, and President Lincoln, refused to wait for military action.

the rebels to return. Lincoln wanted action, and he wanted it soon.

The public agreed; they wanted the rebels punished, the lost land reclaimed. "Forward to Richmond!"[6] the *New York Tribune*'s front page trumpeted day after day, demanding an attack on the Confederate capital.

Defeat at Bull Run

Lincoln urged an offensive against the Confederate forces in Virginia. General Irvin McDowell protested that it was too early. McDowell commanded the Army of the Potomac, the troops stationed around Washington. "This is not an army," he told Lincoln. "It will take a long time to make an army." But Lincoln urged the general on. "You are green, it is true, but they are green, also; you are all green alike."[7] McDowell obeyed orders.

On July 21, the Army of the Potomac attacked the rebels near the Bull Run River. McDowell forgot his own warnings and ordered complicated maneuvers that would have challenged seasoned soldiers. When Confederate reinforcements arrived by train, the Union boys still standing ran back to Washington.

The retreat was panicked chaos. The carriages of Washington socialites who had come to view the war's only battle got tangled in the stream of running soldiers and ambulance wagons. The editor of the *New York Tribune* who had demanded action now promoted giving up: "On every brow sits sullen, scorching, black despair … If it is best for the country and for mankind that we make peace with the rebels, and on their own terms, do not shrink even from that."[8] Hopes for a short war lay trampled with hundreds of bodies in the dirt and blood of the battlefield. But Lincoln would not give up.

CONSTRUCTING A WAR MACHINE

One week after the Battle of Bull Run, Lincoln crouched at his mahogany writing desk. He scribbled several goals: establish the blockade, form a well-disciplined army, protect the capital city, and bring stability to Missouri and the pro-Union portion of Tennessee. Lincoln envisioned all these objectives unfolding at once, stretching the Confederacy's capacity to counteract each effort. The North outmatched the South in all the military statistics: available fighters, financial resources, factories, and infrastructure such as railroad track and telegraph lines. Lincoln needed a war plan that capitalized on these advantages.

Lincoln accompanied this strategizing with an impromptu military education. He studied texts on topics ranging from the philosophical underpinnings of armed conflict to the field commands bellowed by officers. To command the armed forces, Lincoln needed to understand the military world.

An Inventive Approach

One of Lincoln's favorite places was the Washington Navy Yard. In the yard, Lincoln was surrounded by innovative machinery and its makers, a unique class of people with sharp minds and new ideas. His friend John Dahlgren was one of these engineers. He was the nation's premier designer of heavy guns, and Lincoln often asked him for advice on armory.

Lincoln frequently visited the yard to view new technology. He also welcomed inventors to the White House to demonstrate their ideas. When he found a particularly promising design, Lincoln made sure the inventor received a government contract. Lincoln was always interested in any device that had the potential to give Union fighters an advantage in the field or on the seas.

Lincoln's favorite machines to review were breechloading rifled muskets, likely because he could conduct the tests himself. His firing range was the White House's southern lawn, an overgrown patch with a rotting woodpile in its center.

Breechloaders had been invented decades before but were not standard army issue during the war, despite their advantages over the standard musketloaders. Breechloaders were safer and wasted less ammunition, and Lincoln was always eager to try potential improvements to the design. He was, after all, a good shot.

In addition to traditional single-shot rifles, Lincoln took an interest in a new brand of gun, the repeating rifle. Lincoln reviewed and ordered three kinds of these guns—the Springfield, Spencer, and Sharps rifles. Repeaters could fire again and again without reloading, which led the Confederates to think their opponents were a much larger force. The guns were also extremely accurate. A good shooter with a Sharps could hit a target over 500 yards (457 meters) away. Lincoln was so impressed with the Sharps rifle that he commissioned a regiment of marksmen and outfitted them with the gun. The sharpshooters became the best skirmishers in Union ranks.

Lincoln also took an interest in the new and astounding hot air balloons of Thaddeus Lowe. The reconnaissance balloons were outfitted with telegraph transmitters that relayed information to the ground. In 1861, Lowe flew a balloon for the president, sending a telegram to the White House from the sky.

Lincoln thought balloon-acquired intelligence sounded promising, and he endorsed the creation of a balloon corps. By 1862, Lowe's corps flew seven balloons for the Army of the Potomac. At the Battle of Seven Pines, a balloon engineer warned McClellan about General Joseph Johnston's approaching army. Yet McClellan refused to take advantage of this strange, new, sky-high technology. Without evidence that balloon scouting led to Union victories, the balloons ceased flying.

Many witnesses described Lincoln as an overjoyed child during arms demonstrations. The president felt a kinship with inventors and was deeply interested in the way things worked. Yet his promotion of weaponry was more than self-indulgence. It was focused on tipping the scales in the Union's favor. As in other matters, Lincoln was always eager to consider a fresh idea that could help win the war on Union terms.

"Lincoln is the only US president to hold a patent. In 1848, the US Patent and Trademark Office granted Lincoln patent 6469 for a floating mechanism to raise riverboats over sandbars."

The Union Army Balloon Corps gathered intelligence from the sky. The hot air balloon was one of several inventions that Lincoln championed.

Looking for Leadership

Lincoln also attempted to move past Bull Run by putting a new general in charge of the eastern forces. Recognizing his own responsibility in the disaster, the president was quick to reassure General McDowell, "I have not lost a particle of confidence in you."[1] However, Lincoln needed a general who inspired confidence.

The only successful general so far was George McClellan, who had led the campaign to free western Virginia. In late July, Lincoln named McClellan as the commanding officer of the Army of the Potomac and asked the general to submit a plan. One week later, McClellan sent the president twelve pages of recommendations. However, few of them dealt with Washington, DC; Maryland; or Virginia, McClellan's domain. The letter was actually a comprehensive strategy for engaging the rebels in Missouri, Texas, Georgia, Louisiana, and other places under other generals' authority. Some of the items, such as gaining control of the Mississippi River, echoed Lincoln's own objectives, but McClellan had overstepped his bounds, landing right on General Scott's toes.

The next week, McClellan sent a second epistle. This time he warned the president of an impending invasion of the capital and advised that Scott send reinforcements to the city. Scott had had enough. He summoned McClellan, berated him for insulting the general in chief's authority, and challenged his claim that the capital was in danger (the records prove Scott right on this account). After dressing down General McClellan, Scott offered Lincoln his resignation. Lincoln refused. The president pacified Scott, then

General George McClellan's avoidance of bloody conflicts earned him the soldiers' loyalty. His men affectionately dubbed him "Little Mac."

convinced McClellan to withdraw the memo. For the time being, Lincoln had soothed the tension with calm talk, a skill he would call on frequently when other quarrels arose between high-ranking or politically significant officials.

Despite McClellan's arrogance, he was a brilliant organizer. From the sloppy, dirty, and disheartened troops left by McDowell, McClellan sculpted an army that marched with precision, obeyed orders, and kept their camps clean. Yet despite the polish, McClellan kept his men out of battle. Other than a small, failed invasion of northern Virginia in the Battle of Ball's Bluff in October, the eastern troops stayed motionless.

That month, General Scott again submitted his resignation, this time citing declining health. Recognizing McClellan's skill for administration, his compatible vision of fighting many places at once, and the respect he commanded from his men, Lincoln promoted him to replace Scott as general in chief. When Lincoln expressed concern that McClellan would be stretched thin as both general in chief and commander of the Army of the Potomac, McClellan shrugged it off. "I can do it all,"[2] he said.

Sidestepping Slavery

As Lincoln worked to find the right leadership dynamic in the military, he also struggled to find the right balance in his slavery policy. The root of the rebellion was the Southern conviction that Lincoln would damage, limit, or even end the institution. Abolitionists in the North viewed the war as an opportunity to strike down the wicked system and pressured Lincoln to do so. Lincoln detested slavery, but since

Appointing Generals

In the week following Bull Run, Lincoln and Congress requested one million volunteer soldiers. This rapid expansion of the military required the equally rapid appointment of thousands of officers. While soldiers elected company officers and state governors appointed colonels and majors, the president was responsible for naming generals.

Prior to the war, generals came out of West Point, the army's officer academy. At the war's start, West Point graduates received some of the first commissions. Irvin McDowell, the Army of the Potomac's first general, had graduated from West Point, taught at the school, and served in the Mexican War. George McClellan, another West Point alum and Mexican War veteran, had retired from army life for a more lucrative career in the railroads but returned for a major general's commission in 1861. Similarly, Ulysses S. Grant had received a military education at West Point, served in the Mexican War, and left the army in peacetime. When the war started, Grant volunteered to rejoin, first earning an appointment to colonel from the Illinois governor. In July 1861, Lincoln promoted him to brigadier general.

However, there were far more open positions in the Union officer corps than experienced military men. Both the governors and Lincoln solved the shortage by commissioning political leaders with military ranks. This approach also served to gather supporters from multiple factions. Lincoln consolidated his backing from the Republican Party by giving commissions to John Frémont, the first Republican presidential nominee, and Nathaniel Banks, former speaker of the House of Representatives and governor of Massachusetts. Lincoln recruited cooperation from the Democratic

Party by naming Benjamin Butler and John Logan generals. Support from immigrant communities came with appointments for German American politician Franz Sigel and Irishman Thomas Meagher.

Some established generals rued these political appointments. Veteran general Henry Halleck complained, "It seems but little better than murder to give important commands to such men." But he conceded that under the circumstances, "it seems impossible to prevent it."[3] Some of the political generals did fail. Frémont let the Confederates overrun Missouri early in the war and then overstepped his authority by emancipating rebels' slaves. Neither Butler nor Banks distinguished themselves in the field. Yet Logan proved to be an able commander and contributed to the campaigns in Missouri, Tennessee, and Mississippi.

While hopes were higher for the experienced generals, they did not always live up to their résumés. McClellan had graduated second in his West Point class, participated in several victories in the Mexican War, and led the successful liberation of West Virginia in 1861. But he completely failed to merit his quick ascension. During his fourteen months as commander of the Army of the Potomac, McClellan's forces were inactive approximately twelve of those months. In fact, each commander of Union forces in Virginia—McDowell, McClellan, Burnside, Hooker, and Meade—was a career military man, and each disappointed Lincoln.

At the war's outset, Lincoln was forced to commission men who, like himself, were uneducated and inexperienced in military matters. Some of the appointments he regretted—for officers from both political and military backgrounds—and he shuffled officers throughout the war in an attempt to find an effective command structure.

the Constitution approved the system, he did not believe he could act against it.

Yet Lincoln could not keep slavery out of the war. Only a month into the conflict, three slaves snuck away from working on Confederate defenses in Virginia and entered the Union camp at Fortress Monroe. General Benjamin Butler declared that the runaways were contraband of war and were considered seized property of the enemy army. Returning the slaves to their masters would return their labor to the Confederates.

Lincoln made Butler's decision official in August with the First Confiscation Act. The measure authorized Union soldiers to seize rebel property, including freeing slaves working directly for the Confederate military. Lincoln carefully restricted the act so it did not apply to slaves in general. He feared that any hint of freeing slaves, other than as a temporary measure to deprive the enemy of a resource, would drive the border states to the South.

In fact, the same month that Lincoln issued the Confiscation Act, General Frémont declared that all slaves belonging to Confederate sympathizers in Missouri were now free. Lincoln quickly rescinded the order and reprimanded Frémont for acting outside the law. "It is itself the surrender of government. Can it be pretended that it is any longer the government of the U.S.—any government of the Constitution and laws,—wherin a General, or a President, may make permanent rules of property by proclamation?"[4] For now, Lincoln acted conservatively on the slavery issue, hoping that avoiding it would maintain the loyalty of the border states and weaken the secessionist argument. In time, his views on "permanent rules" and "proclamations" would change.

LINCOLN AND THE NAVY

While the navy had its own share of arrogant officers and failed operations, Lincoln had an able leader at the helm. Gideon Welles, with no military or maritime experience, proved a sparkling administrator. Thus, the navy did not require Lincoln's constant oversight, but the president stepped in when he felt it necessary or interesting.

The Blockade

The blockade of Southern ports was one of Lincoln's top objectives, but foreign powers would ignore the blockade if Union ships did not enforce it. As soon as the war started, Welles began ordering new ships and buying private boats. One by one, vessels sailed to Atlantic and Gulf Coast stations. By 1862, the navy had 61,264 ships, half of them converted from merchant craft. These vessels operated the Atlantic and Gulf Blockading Squadrons and seized any ship discovered to be approaching or leaving Southern harbors.

Secretary of the Navy Gideon Welles was one of Lincoln's most trusted advisers.

In addition to ships, the navy needed land bases for blockade operations. The first acquisition was the highly traveled Hatteras Inlet of North Carolina. In August 1861, seven Union ships fired on Forts Clark and Hatteras until the Confederates abandoned them. The next blockade station was obtained in November when Admiral Samuel DuPont's fleet took the island of Port Royal, South Carolina. In addition to providing a prime naval base at the mouth of busy Charleston Harbor, the capture of Port Royal also overturned a long-held military belief. In the time of sail, one cannon on land was considered worth five at sea, making naval attacks on land targets often impractical. However, DuPont's quick and agile steamships evaded much of the fire from the rebels holed up in Fortress Monroe. After DuPont's flotilla pummeled the fort for over four hours, the Confederates evacuated, having damaged—but not disabled—the navy's ships.

With these successes, the anaconda's coils tightened around the Confederacy. Previously, the South exported cotton and other agricultural goods and imported most other products. The blockade threatened this balance. By March 1862, the Confederacy scrounged for war essentials, such as rifles, warships, and gunpowder. Civilians also felt the squeeze. By April 1863, Southerners paid high prices for—or did without—new clothing, weapons, farm equipment, and food.

The USS *Monitor*

The navy was fighting the war at full steam. And it was about to unleash a new kind of ship that would forever alter war at sea.

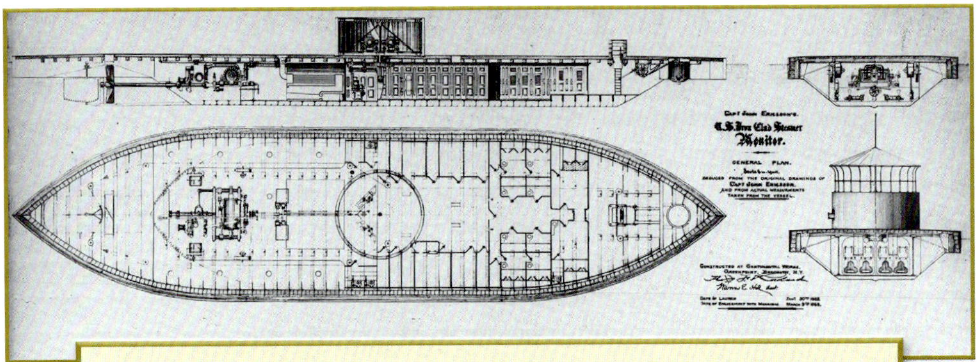

The USS *Monitor* was a new breed of warship. Built of iron and barely rising above the water's surface, the *Monitor* withstood enemy fire at close range.

In the growing light of March 9, 1862, two odd-looking vessels fired on each other near Norfolk, Virginia. A Union sailor described the Confederate's contraption as a "huge, half-submerged crocodile." Yet the Southerners were equally flabbergasted. "There was a craft such as the eyes of a seaman never looked upon before, an immense shingle floating on the water, with a gigantic cheese box rising from its center; no sails, no wheels, no smokestack, no guns. What could it be?"[1] journaled a Confederate.

The ships were the first ironclads. The Confederate's craft, the CSS *Virginia*, had been constructed around the hull of one of the Union ships sunk at Gosport Navy Yard. The rebels had rebuilt the ship and attached a shield of scrap iron. The *Virginia*'s opponent was the USS *Monitor*, just arrived from the New York building yard.

After four hours of blazing guns, the *Virginia* steamed back up the James River. Pits and dents marred both ships, but neither could claim victory in the day's confrontation.

However, the *Monitor* defeated Confederate hopes by keeping the *Virginia* bottled up in the James.

The *Monitor*'s success quieted a panicked tempest in the North. The day before the *Monitor* arrived offshore of Norfolk, the *Virginia* sank two Union ships and ran a third aground. Secretary of War Edwin Stanton lamented that the Southern ship "will change the whole character of the war. She will destroy, *seriatim* [one by one], every naval vessel. She will lay all the cities on the seaboard under contribution."[2]

Yet the *Monitor* would not have been built except for Lincoln's intervention. The navy board in charge of reviewing proposals for ironclads ignored inventor John Ericsson's plan for an iron raft with a rotating gun that shot 166-pound (75.3-kilogram) cannonballs. When another inventor shared Ericsson's innovative design with the president, Lincoln made sure Ericsson got a contract for the ship.

> **"Victory will rest upon the side which holds possession of the seas."**[3]
>
> —*John Ericsson, inventor of the USS* Monitor

The Mighty Union on the Mississippi

As the coastal blockade developed, Lincoln turned his attention to the South's other primary water route—the Mississippi River. Unlike coastal operations, Lincoln could not simply let Welles run the river campaign, because the army traditionally held command over inland waters. Yet operating on such an expansive body of water required the navy's resources. The Mississippi campaign progressed slowly, partly because army officers were reluctant to run a water operation, and there was no command structure for army and navy officials to cooperate. Lincoln circumvented the command problem by taking charge. He managed daily matters, from approving supply orders to orchestrating attacks.

Raining Bombs

One aspect of the Mississippi campaign that particularly captured Lincoln's attention was the invention of a mortar boat, a raft with heavy guns mounted on top that could launch 13-inch (33-centimeter) shells. Lincoln thought the vessels could neutralize the forts along the Mississippi. Because the mortar boats' bombs could hit a target 2 miles (3.2 kilometers) away, the rafts could assault the enemy from around a river bend, out of sight. Mortar boats became a key part of Lincoln's plan to capture New Orleans. However, production lagged under the disorganized operation.

> **"This reminds me of a story," Lincoln said during a discussion about attacking New Orleans. "There was an old woman in Illinois who missed some of her chickens, and couldn't imagine what had become of them. Someone suggested that they had been carried off by a skunk; so she told her husband he must sit up that night and shoot the 'critter.' The old man sat up all**

night and the next day came in with two pet rabbits ... 'Them ain't skunks,' said the old woman ... 'Well then,' returned the old man, 'If them ain't skunks I don't know a skunk when I sees it' ... The navy has been hunting pet rabbits long enough; suppose you send them after skunks."[4]

Lincoln, again, stepped in. He recruited a young navy lieutenant to assist with the project, telling Henry Wise, "Now I am going to devote a part of every day to these mortars, and I won't leave off until it fairly rains Bombs." The president tracked down missing machinery, approved a steamer for crew quarters, ordered ammunition, and ensured that soldiers transferred to the gunboats received wages. Wise admired the president's methodical approach: "He is an evidently practical man, understands precisely what he wants, and is not turned aside by anyone when his work is before him."[5]

New Orleans and Memphis Surrender

Finally, the mortar boats were sent to Admiral David Farragut, the navy officer charged with taking New Orleans. The mortar boats were to take care of the two forts that separated the city from the Gulf of Mexico. For four days, mortars fell on Forts Jackson and St. Philip. The bombs smashed the Confederate positions but did not incapacitate them as planned. Farragut grew impatient. At 2:00 a.m. on April 24, 1862, his ships steamed through the darkness. The forts fired, but the steamships sped through without much damage. Past the forts, Farragut encountered a small fleet of Confederate gunboats but overpowered them.

The next day, Farragut arrived at New Orleans and demanded its surrender. With most of its soldiers in Tennessee opposing Grant, the city did not resist. Not long after, Benjamin Butler and about ten thousand soldiers arrived to occupy the city.

In June, another naval battle captured Memphis, Tennessee. The Union's grip on the Mississippi River had tightened but remained incomplete while the Southerners still held Vicksburg, Mississippi. After winning New Orleans, Farragut had approached Vicksburg but determined that the city on a cliff was impregnable from the water. Lincoln was frustrated with Farragut's assessment. "Vicksburg is the key," the president said. "The war can never be brought to a close until the key is in our pocket."[6]

Lincoln "on the Spot"

Lincoln often visited the front, and in May 1862 he traveled with Chase and Stanton to Fortress Monroe. As the commanding naval officer pointed out the key features of the inlet, including the site of the clash between the *Monitor* and the *Virginia*, Lincoln inquired why the Confederate batteries across the bay at Sewell's Point had been allowed to remain. Likely a little chastened, Rear Admiral Louis Goldsborough arranged for a demonstration against the rebel positions that afternoon.

About noon on May 8, Lincoln boarded a tugboat to follow the six navy steamers commissioned with the attack, including the *Monitor*. He watched as the boats' guns thundered and white smoke mingled with the black smoke from

Admiral David Farragut

By the Civil War, David Farragut had been in the navy over fifty years. In 1810, nine-year-old Farragut had enlisted as a midshipman. Two years later, he commanded a prize ship in South America in the War of 1812. He then patrolled the globe for the next five decades. In 1861, Farragut was in between commands, living in Norfolk, Virginia. The day after Virginia seceded, he moved his wife and son to New York.

Farragut volunteered for active duty, but in the first months of war, there were more officers than ships. Instead, Welles assigned him to the board that reviewed naval officers' loyalty. A year later, Farragut was assigned to command the Gulf Coast Blockading Squadron and to attack New Orleans. To reward Farragut's success in Louisiana, Congress created a new rank of rear admiral.

Farragut's next assignment, however, proved less fruitful. He received orders to cooperate with General Nathaniel Banks to attack Port Hudson, Louisiana. Banks's army would distract the Confederates while Farragut's ships steamed past on the Mississippi. The attack was planned for March 15, 1863. Farragut, however, sailed on the fourteenth. The Confederate gunners forced Farragut to retreat, and Banks's assault the next day also failed. Port Hudson did not surrender for another four months.

Yet Lincoln and Welles had not lost faith, and they commissioned Farragut to attack Mobile Bay,

(continued on the next page)

(continued from the previous page)

Alabama in 1864. This battle secured Farragut's legacy when his fleet captured Fort Morgan and the bay, despite losing a ship to a torpedo. It was in this engagement that Farragut uttered his famous words: "Damn the torpedoes! ... Full speed!"[7] Mobile Bay's capture completed the closure of the Gulf ports.

In between assignments, Farragut enjoyed visiting Washington and attending the many dinners, parties, and other social engagements. He was an occasional guest of both Welles and Lincoln, and a friendship developed between the dynamic seaman and the president. According to Welles, "No man surpasses Farragut in his [Lincoln's] estimation."[8]

the ships' stacks. After a time, the battery's guns quieted, and the Union ships shifted to another battery nearer to the city of Norfolk. However, soon after, a dark plume rose from behind Sewell's Point, and the ships, except the *Monitor,* retreated as the *Virginia* approached. The *Monitor* stood ready for battle, but the *Virginia* turned around.

After receiving confirmation that the rebels had evacuated Sewell's Point, Lincoln asked for a chart of the area. He identified a potential landing spot for the soldiers he wished to advance toward Norfolk. Evidently enjoying the operation, he asked for a boat "to go and see about it on the spot."[9] Thus, the president and two of his advisers sailed to enemy territory to reconnoiter.

The next morning, five thousand soldiers landed on the beach and marched to Norfolk. They were greeted by a delegation that surrendered the city. As the mayor ceremoniously handed over control, the last rebel soldiers evacuated. Crowning the victory, the Confederates made the decision to destroy the *Virginia* in order to keep it out of Union hands.

The city had been vulnerable before Lincoln urged the offensive, with McClellan's troops to the north and other Union troops to the south. Yet, based on the previous caution and reluctance to push the advantage, the Union

Panicked Union officials destroyed the Gosport Navy Yard in Norfolk, Virginia, following Fort Sumter's surrender. The ruins remained when Northern troops retook Norfolk in 1862.

takeover may not have happened without Lincoln's involvement. Chase held to this idea, writing home: "So has ended a brilliant week's campaign of the President; for I think it quite certain that if he had not come down, Norfolk would still have been in possession of the enemy, and the [*Virginia*] as grim and defiant and as much a terror as ever."[10]

COMMANDING THE COMMANDERS

While the navy gained territory in North and South Carolina, Virginia, and Louisiana, the army lay dormant. General in Chief George McClellan drew up plans and promised victories, but he always required more men, more cannons, more supplies. Attorney General Edward Bates urged Lincoln to take a more hands-on approach to the war, "to take and act out the powers of his place, to command the commanders." Bates believed that if the president would "only trust his own good judgment more, and defer less, to the opinions of his subordinates … the affairs of the war and the aspect of the whole country, will be quickly and greatly changed for the better."[1] As Bates desired, Lincoln moved into his position as commander in chief more forcefully in 1862.

A Birthday Present for George Washington

Lincoln's first action of the new year was to replace Secretary of War Simon Cameron with Edwin Stanton, an Ohio lawyer and former attorney general. Stanton, a round man with delicate circle spectacles, possessed a fiery disposition and was ready to take action. Soon after Stanton was sworn in, the White House issued General Order 1, a directive for all forces to attack the enemy by February 22, George Washington's birthday. Instead of plans to comply, Lincoln received protests. Henry Halleck, commander in Missouri, complained he lacked arms and supplies. Lincoln fired back a message that showed his understanding of strategy, an understanding that many of his generals lacked.

"I state my general idea of this war, that we have the greater numbers, and the enemy has the greater facility of concentrating upon points of collision; that we must fail, unless we can find some way of making our advantage an over-match for his; and that this can only be done by menacing him with superior forces at different points, at the same time; so that we can safely attack, one, or both, if he makes no change; and that if he weakens one to strengthen the other, forbear to attack the strengthened one, but seize and hold the weakened one, gaining so much."[2]

Throughout the war, Lincoln struggled to impress the practicality of this approach on his generals.

However, before the deadline arrived, Lincoln once again deferred to McClellan. When the general submitted a proposal for an invasion of the Virginia peninsula, Lincoln rescinded the order. The president also ignored McClellan's previous claim that he could "do it all" and removed him from chief command. Lincoln wanted nothing distracting the reluctant general from success in his own field. Perhaps to not offend McClellan further, Lincoln did not name a replacement. For the next four months, Lincoln acted as his own general in chief. When discussing the situation with Stanton, the two men agreed that they could hardly do a worse job than their predecessors.

The Peninsula Campaign

In March, McClellan landed 121,000 men at Fortress Monroe with all of the supplies, transportation, and support such an operation required. The mass movement showed McClellan's organizational genius, but he seemed satisfied with the successful landing. After a short march up the peninsula, the troops halted at Confederate trenches. McClellan's military education convinced him the 13 miles (21 km) of entrenchment would require tens of thousands of soldiers. Therefore, he decided to siege the city of Yorktown, just across the enemy line, rather than initiate a costly offensive. For the next month, McClellan waited for more and more heavy artillery to arrive.

Lincoln tried to counter McClellan's siege mind-set. He wrote McClellan a letter urging him to attack the enemy, rather than waiting out the enemy at Yorktown: "I think it is the precise time for you to strike a blow—By delay the enemy will relatively gain upon you … It is indispensable to *you* that you strike a blow … I have never written you, or spoken to you, in greater kindness of feeling than now, nor with a fuller purpose to sustain you … *But you must act.*"[3]

Just as McClellan was ready to launch the bombardment on Yorktown, General Albert Johnston pulled the Confederates out. While McClellan believed their numbers outmatched his, the Southerners were in fact outnumbered one to four. The trenches stretched across the peninsula

When McClellan's troops entered the abandoned trenches outside Yorktown, they discovered the cannons were only logs painted black. The Confederates used these "Quaker guns," named after the pacifist Christian group, throughout the war to make their positions appear more heavily armed.

had been mostly empty. "Only McClellan would have hesitated to attack," noted Johnston.[4]

Grant in the West

Further west, Grant's troops continued to succeed. In February, they seized Fort Henry in Kentucky and Fort Donelson in Tennessee, extending Union control of the Tennessee and Cumberland Rivers. The victories also forced Johnston to withdraw the Confederates to a base in Corinth, Mississippi.

In April, Grant's men enjoyed the wildflowers and warm temperatures of the Tennessee spring as they camped in

Edwin Stanton

In January 1862, Lincoln named Edwin Stanton as the new secretary of war. Although the former attorney general had previously criticized Lincoln's administration and characterized Lincoln as unintelligent, calling him "the original gorilla,"[5] he was a capable administrator. Shortly after Stanton's appointment, a senator cautioned Lincoln that the new secretary might try to run away with things. Lincoln responded with a story: We may have to treat him as they are sometimes obliged to treat a Methodist minister I know of out West. He gets wrought to so high a pitch of excitement in his prayers and exhortations that they are obliged to put bricks in his pockets to keep him down. We may be obliged to serve Stanton in the same way, but I guess we'll let him jump a while first. Besides, bricks in his pockets would be better than bricks in his hat.[6]

Stanton was indeed intelligent, as well as energetic, shrewd, and honest. He brought efficiency to the War Department's daily operations and integrity to the business of military contracts. When Lincoln acted as his own top general, Stanton was the president's primary counsel and help.

Over their three and a half years together, Stanton and Lincoln developed a warm friendship.

(continued on the next page)

(continued from the previous page)

Lincoln trusted Stanton with all matters, even when the secretary's hot temper flared at other advisers, generals, or the president himself. Despite their different personalities, the two men shared an affection based on their resolution to see the war through to victory. After the costly Seven Days' Battles in the summer of 1862, McClellan attacked Stanton in the Democratic newspapers, accusing him of "reckless mismanagement and criminal intrigue" that cost "thousands of lives ... thrown away, unnecessarily sacrificed, wantonly squandered, heedlessly murdered." Lincoln vehemently defended his secretary as "a brave and able man" and invited any blame upon himself as commander in chief—where he knew the responsibility ultimately rested.[7]

At the war's conclusion, Stanton submitted his resignation, citing his failing health. Lincoln refused it. "You must help us through the final act. The bag is filled. It must be tied and tied securely. Some knots slip; yours do not," the president said.[8] In fact, Stanton remained a vital part of the White House for several more years. He led the pursuit and trials of John Wilkes Booth and his conspirators after Lincoln's assassination, and he remained secretary of war through the Johnson administration. Confident, crafty, irascible, and resolved, Edwin Stanton proved himself a trustworthy adviser, competent manager, and loyal friend to the president and the nation.

As secretary of war, Edwin Stanton worked with Lincoln daily. The two men developed a strong bond, becoming even closer after they each lost a young son in 1862.

verdant fields at Pittsburg Landing on the Tennessee River and to the west near Shiloh Meeting House. The troops were waiting for another contingent under Don Carlos Buell to arrive before the combined forces attacked the Confederates at Corinth.

On April 6, as Union men cooked breakfast and tidied camp, thirty-five thousand rebels suddenly attacked. By lunchtime, two-thirds of the Union troops had been driven back. The fighting continued into the afternoon, with heavy losses and thousands taken prisoner. The next dawn, however, Grant led a counterattack with the reinforcements just arrived from Buell and another division. Now outmatched, the Confederates retreated to Corinth.

The Southerners had failed to defeat Grant's troops, but the Battle of Shiloh was the bloodiest battle the nation had ever seen; 1,754 Union soldiers perished, and over 8,000 more were wounded. Shocked by the violence, the public criticized Grant. But Lincoln perceived a difference in this general. "I can't spare this man," he said. "He *fights*."[9]

Trouble in the East

McClellan, on the other hand, remained immobile on the peninsula. Therefore, the frustrated president did not hesitate to divert reinforcements headed toward McClellan when he glimpsed an opportunity to surround a contingent of Confederates in Virginia's Shenandoah Valley. In May, the Southern general Stonewall Jackson had defeated Union troops under Frémont and Banks in the valley, just southwest of Washington. Now, Jackson was far from his supply base in Richmond.

The President Sets a Trap

Lincoln wanted Frémont's, Banks's, and McDowell's forces (McClellan's expected reinforcements) to sandwich Jackson and sever him from his supply line. The president sent a flurry of telegrams to the generals with directions, stressing that speed was essential to success. "It is for you, a question of legs," he messaged McDowell. "Put all the speed you can."[10] Despite Lincoln's efforts, Jackson slipped through—Frémont had gone to the wrong place.

Beaten

The day that Jackson escaped Lincoln's trap, General Joseph Johnston attacked two of McClellan's corps that had been separated from the other troops by the rain-swollen Chickahominy River. Reinforcements arrived for both sides, and the Battle of Seven Pines continued throughout the day. The conflict was a draw, but the Confederates stopped McClellan's advance toward Richmond. However, the Southerners also lost their general when Johnston was severely wounded. For the rest of the war, General Robert E. Lee would command the Army of Northern Virginia.

A month later, Lee pursued McClellan in a series of confrontations now called the Seven Days' Battles. McClellan, shaken from seeing the dead after Seven Pines, retreated again and again without counterattacking. Lincoln could see that his general, not his army, was beaten. He ordered McClellan's forces to return to Washington.

The failures in Virginia convinced Lincoln to select a new chief general in hopes of better communicating his vision to commanders in the field. In July, Lincoln ordered Henry Halleck to come to Washington. Halleck was nicknamed "Old Brains" for his expertise on military affairs. He had also overseen Grant's successful campaigns in Tennessee and Kentucky. Lincoln hoped that Halleck's knowledge and experience could put the Union on firmer ground.

> **"I expect to maintain this contest until successful, or till I die, or am conquered. Or my term expires, or Congress or the country forsakes me."**[11]
>
> *—Lincoln to Seward, June 28, 1862*

The Second Battle of Bull Run

In August, General John Pope's troops were stationed in northern Virginia with the double task of protecting the approach to the capital and distracting Lee as McClellan ferried his men off the peninsula. Halleck had ordered McClellan to send the departing soldiers to reinforce Pope, but as always, McClellan stalled. When Lee attacked Pope in late August, McClellan's men had not arrived. Pope ordered counterattack after counterattack, but outnumbered, he eventually retreated toward Washington. Pope's men were defeated physically and emotionally. "Our men are sick of war,"[12] one officer wrote. Lincoln, too, was sickened. One of the cabinet members journaled that the president "seemed wrung by the bitterest anguish."[13]

Halleck was incensed at McClellan's disobedience. "I cannot get General McClellan to do what I wish," he complained to the president, who was disappointed but not surprised.[14] The cabinet called for punishment when it became known that McClellan had ordered approaching reinforcements to halt. Lincoln did not defend his general. "Unquestionably, he has acted badly towards Pope," he said. "He wanted him to fail. That is unpardonable."[15] Yet the president knew that McClellan's men adored the general they referred to as "Little Mac." Removing him would surely plunge morale even lower and could even spark mutiny.

To the consternation of his advisers, Lincoln consolidated Pope's distraught forces with McClellan's, with McClellan over the whole. "He has the slows, is worth little for onward movement," Lincoln conceded, "but beyond any other officer he has the confidence of the army … We must use the tools we have."[16]

Yet Lincoln's available tools were dulling. Only one month into service as general in chief, Halleck had a nervous breakdown, possibly triggered by McClellan's disastrous insubordination. Lincoln did not remove Halleck from position, but the president took back many duties he had handed over in July. Halleck acted as a clerk, adviser, and messenger for the rest of the war, but he did not exercise his command. Lincoln would manage the army himself for the next two years. The president would learn more than he had ever wanted about war and its costs.

NOT BY ARMS ALONE

As the Confederates tallied victories in 1862, Lincoln's disposition toward the rebels hardened. At the beginning of the war, he had hoped to appeal to dormant unionism and reunite the country quickly. Now, with thousands of soldiers sacrificed, he began to use innovative weapons off the battlefield to destroy the South's ability and will to fight on.

Lincoln Suspends Habeas Corpus

Early in his presidency, Lincoln had suspended the writ of habeas corpus in Maryland to keep that state, and its rail lines to the capital, in Union hands. The Constitution provided this power to hold offenders without trial to combat "Rebellion or Invasion."[1] Lincoln also suspended the writ in other small regions as danger arose, before suspending it across the country in September 1862. Military officials could now jail anyone suspected of discouraging enlistment, aiding Confederates, instigating riots, or committing other acts of disloyalty.

The suspension was controversial, but not only because it removed a basic right. The Constitution does not designate who has the right to suspend the writ, and Lincoln's critics asserted that the power belonged to Congress alone. Lincoln's supporters argued that the provision was for emergencies, and therefore the power must rest with the president because Congress is not always in session. Sidestepping the issue, Congress authorized the president's authority "during the present rebellion."[2] Throughout the war, Lincoln maintained he had acted within his role because the suspension of habeas corpus was an essential tool for preserving the Union. "Are all the laws, *but one*, to go unexecuted, and the Government itself go to pieces, lest that one be violated?" he argued.[3]

Lincoln's Slavery Policy

Ever since General Butler had declared that the three slaves who entered his camp in 1861 were contraband, blacks had sought refuge in Union territory. The army managed contraband settlements on islands off the Atlantic coast, providing food, shelter, and clothing for thousands of escaped slaves. While every runaway deprived the Confederacy of a worker, providing for them was costly. Some argued that instead of draining the army of resources, blacks should support it as soldiers.

General Butler himself held this view. When Lincoln sent him to New Orleans in 1862, the general asked the president, "May I arm the Negroes?"

"Not yet, not yet," Lincoln replied.[4]

However, Lincoln did approve of giving blacks noncombatant jobs. The Second Confiscation Act of July

The Lieber Code

In 1862, Stanton and General Halleck commissioned the scholar Francis Lieber to write a code of war, a military rulebook. Lieber was a professor at Columbia University and had published many writings on war. Lieber also believed in a tenet that Lincoln was starting to embrace—"sharp wars are brief."[5]

The first section of the code outlined the principle of military necessity, defined by Lieber as "the necessity of those measures which are indispensable for securing the ends of the war, and which are lawful according to the modern law and usages of war."[6] Within the boundaries of military necessity, Lieber allowed violent acts off the battlefield, such as destruction of civilian property and execution. However, violence for violence's sake was not permitted. In answer to Confederate threats, Lieber forbid the reenslavement or execution of black soldiers. In addition, the code authorized retaliation against enemy captives if black soldiers were mistreated.

Lieber's code also asserted that "war is not carried on by arms alone."[7] The same year Lieber wrote these words, Lincoln drafted the Emancipation Proclamation and the order to nationally suspend habeas corpus. Lincoln viewed both of these measures as necessary to secure the ends of the war.

In 1863, Lincoln approved the code as General Order 100, and Stanton distributed it to all military personnel and Confederate leaders. Lincoln also had the order published in the newspapers. Eventually, the code made its way into other governments' discussions. In 1899, world leaders used Lieber's code as the foundation for an international war treaty, which established the legal authority for the Nazi war crimes trials after World War II. Remnants of the code can also be found in the treaty that governs war today, the Geneva Conventions, instituted in 1949.

The Union Army's contraband policy drew slaves to army camps for protection. Contraband camps sprung up wherever the Union Army arrived.

1862 approved employing escaped slaves "for Military and Naval purposes, giving them reasonable wages for their labor."[8] Yet before the act had passed Congress, Lincoln had something greater than jobs in mind.

Ripening Fruit

Lincoln hated slavery. "If slavery is not wrong, nothing is wrong,"[9] he said. Yet when elected, he asserted that having promised to leave slavery be, he could not abolish it. He followed this conviction in 1861 when he reversed Frémont's order freeing slaves in Missouri and again in May 1862 when General David Hunter made a similar edict in South Carolina, Georgia, and Florida.

Lincoln knew he would have to do something about slavery, but he waited to declare a policy, hoping a clear solution would appear. The president explained his approach to a visitor with a parable: "A man watches his pear-tree day after day, impatient for the ripening of the fruit. Let him attempt to *force* the process, and he may spoil both fruit and tree. But let him patiently *wait*, and the ripe pear at length falls into his lap."[10]

For Lincoln, the guiding principle was whether emancipation would help save the Union. When Horace Greeley's *New York Tribune* openly challenged Lincoln "to consider that Slavery is everywhere the inciting cause and sustaining base of treason," Lincoln answered: "My paramount object in this struggle is to save the Union, and is *not* either to save or to destroy slavery. If I could save the Union without freeing *any* slave, I would do it; if I could save it by freeing *all* the slaves, I would do it; and if I could save it by freeing some and leaving others alone, I would also do that. What I do about slavery and the colored race, I do because it helps save the Union."[11]

In March and July 1862, he presented plans to border state officials for gradual emancipation with government compensation to slave owners. Both times the officials refused to consider the offers. Following the failed July meeting, Lincoln decided that he had given slaveholders enough chances.

On a carriage ride the next day, July 13, he told Welles and Seward, "I have about come to the conclusion that we must free the slaves or be ourselves subdued." When Welles and Seward expressed surprise at Lincoln's policy reversal, he replied, "Well, something must be done."[12] The whole cabinet supported Lincoln's decision, but Seward counseled the president to wait for a military victory. In the present situation of mounting defeat, the move would be seen as "the last shriek on the retreat."[13] Lincoln agreed. He slipped the draft into a desk drawer.

The Battle of Antietam

Confederate gains in 1862 emboldened the rebels, and in September, General Robert E. Lee invaded Pennsylvania and Maryland. The Southerners met McClellan's army near Antietam Creek at Sharpsburg, Maryland, and fiercely resisted repeated Union attacks. The Confederates had only half the Union's force, but McClellan kept troops in reserve instead of seizing the advantage.

The next day, Lee pulled his troops south, and McClellan stayed put despite Lincoln's telegram to "destroy the rebel army if possible."[14] Lincoln was furious and despondent. He believed that McClellan could have ended the war with a decisive battle.

The Proclamation

Yet Northerners celebrated Lee's retreat as a Union victory. Lincoln went along and, on September 22, announced his proclamation that "all persons held as slaves within any State … in rebellion against the United States shall be then, thenceforward, and forever free."[15] Lincoln focused on the act as "a military necessity, absolutely necessary to the preservation of the Union … We must decide whether that element [the slave workforce] should be for us or against us," he told Welles.[16]

Lincoln made frequent trips to visit the armies stationed in the east. In this photograph, he consults with General McClellan before the Battle of Antietam.

> **"We wanted the army to strike more vigorous blows. The administration must set the army an example and strike at the heart of the rebellion."**[17]
>
> —*Abraham Lincoln*

The Army Attacks

Having struck his blow, Lincoln hungered for military success. He ordered McClellan to cross into Virginia and attack Lee. As usual, McClellan made excuses about being unequipped. After another wasted month, Lincoln replaced McClellan with General Ambrose Burnside.

Catastrophe at Fredericksburg

Burnside immediately crafted a plan to approach Richmond by first taking Fredericksburg, halfway between the two capitals. The army would cross the Rappahannock River from the north and charge Fredericksburg. Lincoln was skeptical but decided to try his new general. Halleck would order the supplies needed to erect pontoon bridges over the Rappahannock.

On November 14, 1862, 110,000 soldiers marched toward Fredericksburg. Pleased with the quick movement, Lincoln dared to hope he had found his general at last. Yet when the troops reached the Rappahannock, they found no bridge-building supplies. Halleck had not sent them.

By the time the engineers constructed the bridges, over seventy-two thousand rebel soldiers waited from fortified positions. Half the Southern forces perched atop Marye's Heights, a hill overlooking the city. Wave after wave of soldiers in blue barreled up the hill only to be shot down by the Confederate artillery hunkered behind a stone wall. The Confederate position was unassailable from Burnside's frontal attack. The Army of the Potomac suffered 13,353 casualties in the four-day Battle of Fredericksburg. "If there is a worse place than hell, I am in it,"[18] Lincoln said when he received the report.

The disaster at Fredericksburg decimated the army's morale, and the number of desertions swelled. Lincoln removed Burnside and appointed Joseph Hooker in his place to try to restore spirits. "Give us victories,"[19] he charged the new commander.

Stalemate in Tennessee

Generals elsewhere in the country also struggled to produce results. After replacing Buell in Tennessee, General William Rosecrans initially defeated Confederate forces under Braxton Bragg at the Battle of Stones River over the New Year's holiday. While the victory gave Northern morale a much needed boost following Fredericksburg, Rosecrans did not press his advantage. He held his position but ignored frequent Confederate cavalry raids. A long stalemate set in.

Freedom Fighters

Despite the Union's precarious footing in the war, Lincoln followed through with the Emancipation Proclamation on January 1, 1863. He cited "the power in me vested as Commander-in-Chief, of the Army and Navy of the United States" and promised that the authority of the government and military would protect the bequeathed freedom.[20]

With the final document sitting before him awaiting his signature, Lincoln reflected: "I never in my life felt more certain that I was doing right than I do in signing this paper … If my name ever goes into history it will be for this act, and my whole soul is in it … The south had fair warning that if they did not return to their duty, I should strike at

President Lincoln is shown signing the Emancipation Proclamation, surrounded by cabinet members.

this pillar of their strength. The promise must now be kept, and I shall never recall one word."

Then, with a few confident strokes, he penned his name. "That will do," he said.[21]

The proclamation was not a simple declaration of freedom for slaves. In freeing only the slaves in rebel-held areas, it effectively freed no one. Slaves in the border states and areas under Union control, such as New Orleans, were unaffected. The promised freedom depended wholly on ultimate Union victory, which as 1863 dawned, looked uncertain at best.

At the time, the proclamation's significance lay with the altered approach it represented. For nearly two years, Lincoln had asserted he would not touch slavery. Now, he thrust emancipation to the top of his war objectives. And while the proclamation did not immediately end slavery, it was the death knell of the institution.

The revised proclamation also stated that former slaves would be "received into the armed service of the United States to garrison forts, positions, stations, and other places, and to man vessels of all sorts in said service."[22] Blacks could now bear arms and fight to ensure their freedom. Recruiting black soldiers turned out to be a pivotal maneuver. Over the next twenty-seven months, two hundred thousand blacks donned Union uniforms.

By the end of 1862, the Union had suffered high casualties at Shiloh, Seven Pines, Second Bull Run, Antietam, and Fredericksburg. Democrats had capitalized on the country's sorrow in the November election, gaining twenty-eight seats in the House of Representatives. Yet there had also been progress. The Union controlled regions in Tennessee, Louisiana, and Virginia. The navy dominated most of the Mississippi River, and the blockade cinched ever tighter. Furthermore, Lincoln's gamble on emancipation had not unraveled the war or the White House. As 1863 began, the "worn & haggard"[23] president could only hope that the blows he'd leveraged would begin to bear fruit.

PERSEVERANCE AND SACRIFICE

In April 1863, Lincoln met with General Hooker. The president emphasized that "our prime object is the enemies' army in front of us, and is not with, or about Richmond." Lincoln also counseled Hooker to use all his resources. Remembering that some troops had stayed on the sidelines at Antietam and Fredericksburg, Lincoln advised Hooker, "In your next fight, put in all your men."[1] If Hooker had heeded this wisdom, his plan may have turned out differently.

The Battle of Chancellorsville

Hooker had spent the four months since Fredericksburg training, drilling, and restoring the pride of his troops. Now, he wanted to renew the attack on Fredericksburg, but from behind the Confederate positions. On April 30, Hooker's cavalry destroyed Confederate railroads while the infantry crossed the Rappahannock River and encircled

Fredericksburg. However, Stonewall Jackson's corps arrived unexpectedly, and Hooker pulled back to the village of Chancellorsville.

The Confederates attacked on three subsequent days and eventually drove the Union forces back over the river. Contrary to Lincoln's advice, Hooker had used only one-third of his forces. On hearing the result, Lincoln's depression thickened. "He looks exhausted, care-worn, spiritless, extinct," noted a state department worker.[2]

When Lee's forces marched into Pennsylvania a month later, Hooker demanded more troops to meet the threat. Halleck insisted none could be spared. In a symbolic gesture of protest, Hooker resigned, likely expecting that Lincoln would insist he stay on. But Lincoln did not insist. He had "observed in Hooker the same failings that were observed in McClellan after the battle of Antietam—a want of alacrity to obey, and a greedy call for more troops which could not, and ought not to be taken from other points."[3] General George Meade became the Army of the Potomac's fifth commander.

> **"We cannot help beating them if we have the man."**[4]
>
> — *Abraham Lincoln*

The Battle of Gettysburg

Just three days after receiving command, Meade moved his army to a position between the rebels and Washington. Lee gathered his forces at Gettysburg, Pennsylvania. From July 1 to 3, the two armies fought in the town of Gettysburg and over the southern hills. Meade's forces gained strategic positions and repulsed a Confederate charge. At last, the Confederates withdrew, leaving over fifty-one thousand casualties. The Battle of Gettysburg was a solid Union victory, but a victory at great cost. Still, relief swept the North. One citizen journaled, "The army of the Potomac has at last found a general that can handle it."[5]

The Siege of Vicksburg

As cannons boomed in Gettysburg, another contest was drawing to a close. In the spring of 1863, General Grant and Admiral David Dixon Porter had begun a joint operation

The Battle of Gettysburg ended General Lee's boldest push into Northern territory. Today, the battlefield is a national military park.

against Vicksburg, Mississippi. Grant won five battles in the surrounding swamps, but his two attacks on the city failed. A siege developed, with Grant's men sealing off the city from land and Porter's squadron bombarding it from the river. For a month, Vicksburg's residents lived in earthen tunnels and watched their food supplies dwindle.

Finally, on July 4, Vicksburg surrendered. The key to the Mississippi was finally in the president's pocket. When Lincoln received the news, joy overcame his lean frame. He wrapped Welles in his long arms and squeezed.

Five days later, Port Hudson, Louisiana, received news of Vicksburg's defeat and surrendered to General Banks, ending a six-week siege. The Mighty Mississippi was now completely in Union control, and the Confederacy was sliced in two.

Incomplete Work

Immediately after hearing of Vicksburg's capture, Lincoln wired Meade, who was still near Lee's army after Gettysburg. "Vicksburg surrendered to General Grant on July 4. Now, if General Meade can complete his work, so gloriously begun so far, by the literal or substantial destruction of Lee's army, the rebellion will be over."[6]

Soon after, Lincoln received a copy of a letter from General Meade to his soldiers. It congratulated the forces on victory at Gettysburg and encouraged them "to drive from our soil every vestige of the presence of the invader." Lincoln fumed to his secretary John Hay, "Drive the invaders from our soil! Great God! Is that all? … Will our Generals never get that idea out of their heads? The whole country is *our* soil."[7] As Meade's letter foretold, he

Vicksburg sits on a high bluff at a sharp bend in the Mississippi River. The city frustrated both the Union Army and Navy. Vicksburg resisted a month of assaults and a six-week siege before finally surrendering to Northern forces.

did not lead a counterattack, and Lee withdrew his troops overnight. When Lincoln learned that Lee was safely in Virginia, he relinquished all hope of the war ending quickly. "We had them within our grasp. We had only to stretch forth our hands and they were ours."[8] For the rest of 1863, only small skirmishes occurred between the armies in Virginia.

The Gettysburg Address

After the Battle of Gettysburg, the governor of Pennsylvania bought 17 acres (6.9 hectares) of the battlefield for a burial ground for the conflict's fallen. For the cemetery's dedication, the governor invited renowned orator Edward Everett and President Lincoln to speak. On November 19, 1863, Everett spoke for two hours; Lincoln spoke for two minutes. Everett's words are rarely recalled, while Lincoln's short soliloquy is still recited. The president evoked the Declaration of Independence and its values of liberty and equality, framing the war as a battle for freedom. He called on the nation to honor the dead by achieving the goal for which they had sacrificed.

> Four score and seven years ago our fathers brought forth on this continent, a new nation, conceived in Liberty, and dedicated to the proposition that all men are created equal.
>
> Now we are engaged in a great civil war, testing whether that nation, or any nation so conceived and so dedicated, can long endure. We are met on a great battle-field of that war. We have come to dedicate a portion of that field, as a final resting place for those who here gave their lives

that that nation might live. It is altogether fitting and proper that we should do this.

But, in a larger sense, we can not dedicate —we can not consecrate—we can not hallow—this ground. The brave men, living and dead, who struggled here, have consecrated it, far above our poor power to add or detract. The world will little note, nor long remember what we say here, but it can never forget what they did here. It is for us the living, rather, to be dedicated here to the unfinished work which they who fought here have thus far so nobly advanced. It is rather for us to be here dedicated to the great task remaining before us—that from these honored dead we take increased devotion to that cause for which they gave the last full measure of devotion—that we here highly resolve that these dead shall not have died in vain—that this nation, under God, shall have a new birth of freedom—and that government of the people, by the people, for the people, shall not perish from the earth.

Abraham Lincoln
November 19, 1863[9]

Meanwhile, Union troops landed on Morris Island, to the south of Charleston Harbor. On July 11, they took over some Confederate defenses but could not flush the rebels from Fort Wagner on the island's northern tip. A week later, the Yankees renewed the attack. After a barrage from both land artillery and navy gunners, the black soldiers of the Fifty-Fourth Massachusetts Colored Infantry led a charge toward the fort. Some troops survived the heavy fire to scale the fort walls. They engaged in fierce hand-to-hand combat with the defenders but could not wrest the fort from the rebels.

The defeat at Charleston and Meade's failure to destroy Lee's army drained the confidence that had followed Gettysburg and Vicksburg. Having glimpsed peace, these failures hung even heavier on Lincoln's sagging shoulders.

Black Soldiers and Their Loyal Commander

Although the attack on Fort Wagner failed, the Fifty-Fourth Massachusetts's courage earned respect for black soldiers. Likewise, during the Vicksburg Campaign, black troops in the First Mississippi, Ninth Louisiana, and Eleventh Louisiana had defended Grant's supply depot from attack. Black troops fought with distinction in Missouri, Louisiana, Virginia, and beyond.

Yet arming blacks was controversial. Many white Americans believed that blacks were incapable of the bravery, resourcefulness, and grit required of a soldier. However, the more battles that included black soldiers, the fewer the detractors numbered. A journalist traveling with Grant's

The Fifty-Fourth Massachusetts relentlessly attacked Fort Wagner but failed to evict the Southern defenders. For his heroism in the battle, Sergeant William H. Carney became the first African American to earn the Congressional Medal of Honor.

troops in Mississippi commented, "The bravery of the blacks completely revolutionized the sentiment of the army with regard to the employment of negro troops. I heard prominent officers who formerly in private had sneered at the idea of negroes fighting express themselves after that as heartily in favor of it."[10]

While black soldiers tangibly contributed in battle, their presence had a cost. After the Battle of Fort Wagner, the rebels refused to release black soldiers with white prisoners. This directly violated the Lieber Code's principle of equal treatment for all prisoners of war. The Confederates also announced that any former slaves captured as Union soldiers would be returned to slavery or executed.

In response, Lincoln suspended prisoner exchanges. The president also threatened to retaliate against Confederate prisoners of war for any black soldiers executed or reenslaved—but his heart never allowed it. Lincoln confessed that "the thought of hanging men for a crime perpetrated by others was revolting."[11] Nevertheless, Southerners did not hesitate to execute captured black soldiers. On April 12, 1864, Confederate soldiers gunned down black troops attempting to surrender at Fort Pillow, Tennessee. Black soldiers were also murdered in Louisiana, Arkansas, and North Carolina.

Lincoln did not retaliate, but he refused to reinstate prisoner exchanges despite intense criticism for allowing thousands of white soldiers to languish in prisoner-of-war camps. In Lincoln's view, black soldiers had fulfilled their pledge to the nation, and he would fulfill his promise to protect them as best he could.

Freeing Tennessee

As black troops increased the Union's manpower advantage, new technology increased soldiers' effectiveness. In 1863, repeating rifles appeared in troops' hands, a result of Lincoln's enthusiasm for innovation. The guns played a key role in the Battle of Gettysburg and in General Rosecrans's takeover of east Tennessee.

Besieged

Rosecrans's Army of the Cumberland used Spencer rifles to force Braxton Bragg's Confederates out of Chattanooga,

Tennessee, on September 9. The guns sounded again ten days later when George Thomas held off a Confederate assault while Rosecrans and the rest of the Army of the Cumberland made it safely back to Chattanooga. Bragg had stopped the Union advance, but he had not destroyed Rosecrans's army or retaken Chattanooga as planned. Instead, the Southern general surrounded the city and cut off incoming supplies. The Army of the Cumberland hunkered down and tallied provisions.

Rosecrans's difficulties were partly because of poor coordination between western troops. Lincoln had encouraged cooperation, but the commanders continued to operate independently. Finally, in October 1863, Lincoln combined all western commands into the Military Division of the Mississippi. He put the one general who had not yet disappointed him in charge—Ulysses S. Grant. Lincoln ordered Grant to break the siege on Chattanooga before Rosecrans and his men starved.

Grant's Breakthrough

Grant immediately replaced Rosecrans with Thomas. He had learned that Rosecrans planned to retreat and surrender the city, an unacceptable abdication of a hard-fought strategic position. Second, Grant opened a supply line into the city by taking a lightly guarded road through a narrow pass. Then in November, Grant attacked. Over three days, the Union drove Bragg's forces into Georgia.

Finally, after two years, the pro-Union citizens of eastern Tennessee were in Union territory. Lincoln sent Grant "my more than thanks—my profoundest gratitude."[12]

This drawing of the area around Chattanooga, Tennessee, in 1863 shows Confederate fortifications, Union and Confederate picket lines, railroads, roads, and waterways.

The North would use its hard-fought position to mount key Union movements in the following year.

Reconstruction in the West

By the close of 1863, the Union controlled territory in Louisiana, Arkansas, Mississippi, Alabama, and Tennessee. To manage these areas, Lincoln announced the Proclamation of Amnesty and Reconstruction. The Ten Percent Plan, as it was nicknamed, was the first step to reinstating Southerners into the United States. The program allowed Southern states to set up pro-Union governments if 10 percent of voters swore loyalty to the Union. The plan also offered amnesty to any participants of the rebellion who now swore the oath. For the rest of the war, Louisiana and Arkansas operated under this system.

GRANT TAKES CHARGE

As the campaigning season and the election season of 1864 approached, Lincoln again sought a general to take charge. The president needed to turn the war around if he were to win reelection in November.

One general stood out. Ulysses S. Grant had secured difficult victories in Mississippi and Tennessee, obeyed orders he didn't like, and never complained of limited resources. In March, Lincoln summoned Grant to Washington and gave him supreme command. The two men had never before met, but they instantly liked one another. Lincoln told Grant that "all he wanted or had ever wanted was someone who would take the responsibility and act."[1] Lincoln did not even care to know Grant's plans. Sensing he could trust the victor of Forts Henry and Donelson, Vicksburg, and Chattanooga, Lincoln relinquished control.

The Plan

Grant, however, submitted a comprehensive plan one week later. The general envisioned a three-pronged attack led by himself and two generals who had served beside him at Chattanooga. William Tecumseh Sherman would march across the Deep South against Joseph Johnston, who had replaced Bragg following the siege of Chattanooga. Grant ordered Sherman to destroy crops, factories, cities, and rail and telegraph lines. Sherman would eliminate Confederate resources and break the South's resolve to fight. Philip Sheridan would lead the Cavalry Corps through the Shenandoah Valley, flushing out the rebel cavalry commanded by Jubal Early. Sheridan would also destroy Southern resources, including the fertile valley's troop-sustaining crops. Grant would station himself with General Meade in Virginia. The Army of the Potomac would assail Lee's army until it was destroyed.

Lincoln must have been elated. Finally, a general grasped his vision of coordinated attacks that would stretch the Southern army to a breaking point. Furthermore, only six weeks later, all three armies marched toward the enemy.

With Grant behind the reigns, Lincoln disentangled himself from hour-by-hour military involvement. When Welles asked advice on the joint campaign to take Wilmington, North Carolina, Lincoln responded, "I must refer you to General Grant."[2]

Grant Gets His Teeth In

The year's first engagement between Meade's Army of the Potomac and Lee's Army of Northern Virginia occurred at the Battle of the Wilderness. On May 4, Lee attacked the south-moving federals in dense thickets. In two days of fighting, the Union lost over eighteen thousand men, but Grant continued the march.

The Battle of the Wilderness was the first conflict of Grant's Overland Campaign in Virginia. It would be a bloody drive to Richmond for Union troops and their Southern opponents.

Lincoln may have held his breath upon hearing of the defeat. Under similar circumstances, each of Grant's predecessors had retreated north. Grant, however, assured the president, "There is to be no turning back." After another two days of fighting, Grant wired, "I propose to fight it out on this line if it takes all summer."[3]

> **"He has the grit of a bull-dog! Once let him get his 'teeth' in, and nothing can shake him off ... It is the dogged pertinacity of Grant that wins."**[4]
>
> —*Lincoln to John Hay after the Battle of the Wilderness*

After another two weeks of fighting near Spotsylvania Courthouse, Grant swung the troops in a southern arc around Richmond to approach Petersburg. Petersburg lay south of Richmond and hosted the Confederate's railroad supply line. When Lincoln learned of the move, he telegrammed his encouragement. "I begin to see it," he wrote Grant. "You will succeed."[5]

At first, Northern troops pushed Southerners out of their positions southeast of Petersburg in successive engagements on June 15–17. But on the fourth day, Southern reinforcements fended off further attacks. Grant now realized only a siege would extricate the Confederates from their trenches, and he positioned troops to seal off Southern supplies. Lincoln wired Grant: "Hold on with a bull-dog grip, and chew & choke, as much as possible." When the general read the message, "he broke into a hearty laugh" and said, "The President has more nerve than any of his advisors."[6]

Attack on Washington

Trying to distract Grant from Petersburg, Lee sent Jubal Early to menace Washington, DC. In July, Early's troops moved into Maryland and approached Washington from the northwest. Union forces resisted Early's advance at the Monocacy River but could not repel the Southerners. Early arrived at the capital's edge on July 11. Yet the delay at Monocacy gave reinforcements time to arrive. When Early realized veteran troops from the Army of the Potomac were filling positions around the city, he abandoned the attack.

General Grant's humble manner distinguished him from the other high-ranking generals. He prized victory rather than position and went after success with a bulldog's tenacity.

General Ulysses S. Grant

Ulysses S. Grant's talent for command should not have come as a surprise. The general had graduated from West Point and served in the Mexican War, earning commendations for bravery and exemplary conduct.

Yet his success did not survive peacetime. The army shipped Grant to Oregon Territory to police the tense situation between settlers and Native Americans. Then it sent him to California. In both positions, he was separated from his wife, Julia, and his children. Grant struggled with loneliness and alcoholism. In 1854, he was forced to resign.

At last he was home with Julia, but he struggled to make a living. He tried farming, collecting bills, and selling leather goods. Grant failed at them all, and the family struggled to pay its expenses.

When the Civil War started, Grant immediately rejoined the army. He pleased the president right away with the peaceful capture of Paducah, Kentucky, in September 1861. His successes at Forts Henry and Donelson in Tennessee the next year earned Grant the nickname "Unconditional Surrender."

Grant also won respect for his simple ways. While traveling with Grant's army in Mississippi, Representative Elihu Washburne wrote Lincoln. "I am afraid Grant will have to be reproved for want of style," Washburne quipped. "On this whole march for five days he has had neither a horse nor

(continued on the next page)

(continued from the previous page)

an orderly or servant, a blanket or overcoat or clean shirt, or even a sword ... His entire baggage consists of a tooth-brush."[7]

Despite Grant's early victories in Kentucky, calls came for his removal after the bloody Battle of Shiloh and during the long Vicksburg campaign. During the quagmire in Mississippi, Grant's opponents wrote editorials in the newspapers, penned letters to Lincoln, and even called on the president in person to demand Grant's removal. But Lincoln stood by the general. Grant had promised to capture Vicksburg by July 4; the president believed him.

And right on schedule, Vicksburg surrendered. The city's fall was a turning point, for both the war and Grant. His critics fell silent as he defeated the enemy at Chattanooga and then chased Lee across Virginia. Lincoln at last removed himself from daily military affairs, trusting Grant in every matter. For his part, Grant consulted Lincoln when politics and military affairs collided.

Where other generals in Virginia had given up in discouragement, Grant gritted his teeth and pressed the enemy until it ran out of places to run. Criticism resurfaced during the costly Virginia campaign but died down again after Appomattox. The nation elevated Grant to the status of hero and elected him president in 1868. When Grant died in 1885, he was buried in New York City in a massive, elaborate tomb, reminiscent of the capitol building. The site is now a national memorial.

> **"Lincoln is the only sitting president to be in the midst of a battle. He viewed Early's attack from the walls of Fort Stevens."**

Sherman in Georgia

Meanwhile, Sherman's forces entered Georgia and gradually pushed by Johnston's troops. The armies met in May at the Battle of Resaca and in June at the Battle of Kennesaw Mountain. Displeased with Johnston's steady retreat, Confederate president Jefferson Davis sent John Bell Hood to take over the Confederate troops.

In July, Hood confronted Sherman outside Atlanta in two battles, but the rebels failed to dislodge the Union forces from their positions surrounding the city. Sherman severed the last remaining rail line into Atlanta, forcing Hood to evacuate on the night of September 1. The next day, Sherman's forces moved in. With Sherman's success in Georgia and the successful repulse of Early's attack, Northern morale lifted. For the first time that year, Lincoln's reelection in November seemed possible.

Sheridan in the Shenandoah

During the Battle of Spotsylvania Courthouse, Sheridan's cavalry of twelve thousand rode south toward Richmond, drawing away the Confederate cavalry under J. E. B. Stuart. On May 11, the two cavalries faced off at Yellow Tavern. Around midday, the First Virginia Cavalry charged into the Union troops accompanying Sheridan. As a Michigan regiment retreated, a private noticed Stuart in his yellow sash and plumed hat. The private aimed and fired, and Stuart collapsed on his horse. The Confederates stopped Sheridan's advance, but they lost a daring leader. Stuart died the following day.

In September, Sheridan moved into the Shenandoah Valley. His forces defeated Early's troops in two battles and then destroyed everything in their path. They burned barns and mills and tore apart factories and railroads. Sheridan's men left 400 square miles (1,036 sq km) of the valley useless.

The next month, Early tried once more to stop Sheridan. The Confederates attacked at Cedar Creek, Virginia, and drove away three Union corps while Sheridan was 10 miles (16 km) away in Winchester. When he heard of Early's attack, Sheridan galloped to the battlefield. The general bolstered his troops and led a fierce counterattack that drove Early out of the valley for good.

Votes for Victory

As Grant, Sherman, and Sheridan labored to dismantle the Confederate Army, the presidential election campaign unfolded. The Republicans had renominated Lincoln on a "No Peace Without Victory"[8] platform. The Democratic Party nominated Lincoln's failed general, George McClellan. McClellan announced he would do anything to end the war, including giving the rebels independence. A Boston newspaper voiced the Democrats' views: "The Confederacy perhaps can never really be beaten … it is time to agree to a peace without victory."[9] "Stop the War!"[10] cried another paper supporting McClellan.

As part of their peace campaign, the Democrats claimed that the South would rejoin the Union if Lincoln dropped his emancipation policy. The president decided to demonstrate their error. In July, he sent two officials to offer peace to Jefferson Davis on the previously stated terms of reunion, emancipation, and amnesty. As Lincoln hoped, Davis obliterated the Democrats' claim. "We are fighting for Independence—and that, or extermination, we will have," retorted Davis. "You may 'emancipate' every negro in the Confederacy, but we will be free."[11]

In addition to publicizing Davis's response in the newspapers, Lincoln answered the critics by highlighting the contributions of black soldiers and confirming his resolution to fulfill the promise of emancipation. "If [black soldiers] stake their lives for us they must be prompted by the strongest motive—even the promise of freedom. And the promise being made, must be kept."[12]

Yet many Northerners respected Lincoln's determination. The victory platform particularly resonated with soldiers. "We want peace too," wrote one serviceman, "*honorable* peace, won in the full light of day at the bayonet's point, with our grand old flag flying over us as we negotiate it."[13] Another soldier encouraged his comrades to support Lincoln: "Give the rebellion another thump this fall by voting for Old Abe. I cannot afford to give three years of my life to maintaining this nation and then give the Rebels all they want."[14]

By the time Election Day arrived on November 8, Sherman had taken Atlanta, and Sheridan had defeated Early in the Shenandoah Valley. In addition, Admiral Farragut had captured Mobile Bay. These successes

Father Abraham's Soldiers

The Pennsylvania militiamen were the first reinforcements in Washington after Fort Sumter fell. Upon their arrival, Lincoln visited their makeshift quarters in the capitol building's basement. The unit had been attacked by a mob while crossing the city of Baltimore, and the men were nursing wounds and receiving weapons when Lincoln descended the shadowed stairway. Moved by their loyalty, he announced, "I have come to give you a warm welcome to the city of Washington and to shake every officer and soldier by the hand."[15]

From the beginning, Lincoln regularly visited his men. He made weekly trips to the Soldiers' Home in Washington, frequently visited the nearby camps and forts, and took any opportunity to show his appreciation to a veteran. After hearing that the *Monitor*'s commander was injured in the ironclad's clash with the *Virginia* in 1862, Lincoln rushed to the lieutenant's lodging. When the officer said he was greatly honored by the visit, Lincoln replied, "No, sir, you have done me and your country honor."[16]

Lincoln was a relatable commander in chief. Soldiers appreciated his warm gaze and firm handshake, and many of them shared his pastoral beginnings in poverty. The president often greeted a soldier as "my son," and the ranks began to call him "Father Abraham."

Lincoln's kindness toward soldiers in trouble increased the men's affection. He welcomed any excuse to spare a life, and his tendency to issue pardons for soldiers sentenced to death for desertion or dereliction of duty became well known. When in doubt about a case, Lincoln would postpone the punishment until he could investigate. "I must put this by until I can settle in my mind whether this soldier can better serve the country dead than living," he would say.[17]

Lincoln's personable manner, his oft-expressed gratitude for his men's sacrifices, and his compassion forged a sturdy bond between the commander in chief and his men at arms. This relationship proved instrumental in pressing the war to its conclusion.

boosted the nation's confidence that Lincoln could in fact win the war. Buoyed by 78 percent of the soldier vote, Lincoln prevailed.

"LET THE THING BE PRESSED"

With Lincoln's second term secured, the army continued Grant's plan. The election assured the commanders their efforts would not be wasted, but the next five months would be grueling.

The March to the Sea

One week after Lincoln's reelection, Sherman's troops left Atlanta. One contingent would move toward the Atlantic coast, executing Grant's orders "to get into the interior of the enemy's country as far as you can, inflicting all the damage you can against their war resources."[1] The other division, under George Thomas, would contain Hood's forces.

As Sherman departed Atlanta, he destroyed bridges, roads, and railroad tracks. His men would not need a supply line; they would live off the food in Southern fields, barns, and kitchens. The foraging parties, known as bummers,

As Sherman's men marched through the South, they pried up and bent railroad rails to make them unusable for reconstruction.

became adept at finding food buried in a yard, keepsakes hidden in hollow trees, and cotton bales concealed in hay.

Sherman also ordered all telegraph lines dismantled. This would keep Confederates from wiring warnings of Sherman's movements. It also kept the general from reporting to Grant or Lincoln. The president would hear nothing from Sherman for a month. Yet Lincoln gathered from Southern newspapers that Sherman was succeeding at terrifying the Southerners.

Occasionally, Sherman's men encountered small bands of Confederates, but the Southern forces were too weak to pose a real threat. The only true battle came at Griswoldville, on November 22, when Union repeating rifles dismantled a Southern militia charge. When the shooting ceased, the federal soldiers recoiled at seeing the bodies of teenage boys and elderly men. The South was running out of soldiers.

Sherman's specter haunted the South. Citizens did not know when to expect him or whether their property would be ransacked or ignored. Rumors spread of violence, but there were few actual reports of soldiers harming citizens. In fact, Sherman hoped the brutal march would save lives by quickening the war's end.

> **"War, at best, is terrible, and this war of ours, in its magnitude and duration, is one of the most terrible ... We accepted this war for an object, a worthy object, and the war will end when that object is attained."**[2]
>
> —*Abraham Lincoln*

A Christmas Present for the President

Finally, Sherman reemerged outside Savannah. On December 21, the mayor handed over the city. Sherman wired Lincoln: "I beg to present to you as a Christmas gift the city of Savannah."[3]

As soon as the city surrendered, the punishment stopped. Sherman shared the army's provisions with the residents and ordered his favorite military band to play a fleeing politicians. Where Sherman met no resistance, he inflicted no suffering.

Final Tasks

Meanwhile, Thomas tore at Hood's army in Georgia and pursued the Confederates to Nashville. Finally, on December 15, Hood launched a full-scale assault. With double the number of Hood's men, the federals drove the Southerners away from the city and dismantled their ranks. The Confederate Army of the Tennessee would not fight again.

That winter also marked the completion of the blockade. In January, a joint operation captured North Carolina's Fort Fisher. The Union victory closed Wilmington, the South's last open East Coast port. For the first time, Southerners talked about peace.

The Hampton Roads Conference

By the close of 1864, Sherman's troops had desolated Georgia. Sheridan had charred the Shenandoah Valley. Furthermore, Southern armies were disintegrating.

In February, Jefferson Davis sent peace emissaries. Lincoln again offered the familiar terms:

1. The restoration of the National authority throughout all the States.
2. No receding by the Executive of the United States, on the Slavery question …
3. No cessation of hostilities short of an end of the war, and the disbanding of all forces hostile to the government.[4]

The officials refused and returned to Davis.

The Peacemakers by George Healy shows a meeting between *(from left to right)* Sherman, Grant, Lincoln, and Porter on March 28, 1865. The leaders discussed terms for the approaching peace aboard the *River Queen* near Grant's headquarters at City Point, Virginia.

Closing In

The rebels needed more convincing, but Sherman and Grant were up to the task. In February 1865, Sherman resumed his march, this time through the Carolinas. Union soldiers paid special attention to stripping South Carolina, where the rebellion had spawned. On February 17, they captured the capital, Columbia. On the same day, the Confederates evacuated Charleston, and Fort Sumter returned to federal control.

By March, Grant's troops had been encamped around Petersburg and Richmond for nine months. As the ground thawed, Lee's men subsisted on dried corn and struggled to mend their threadbare uniforms.

Lee knew he would lose if the federals attacked. Therefore, he commissioned General John Gordon to find a weak spot in the Union lines and launch a full-scale offensive. Lee hoped to extricate his men from Petersburg. Gordon identified the target—Fort Stedman, an earthen fortification with 9-foot (2.7-m) dirt-and-log walls and a few peripheral batteries. If the assault succeeded, the Confederates would march toward Grant's headquarters at City Point, 10 miles (16 km) away.

Lee's Last Try

In the icy predawn of March 25, the Confederate army snuck into the dry cornfield in front of Fort Stedman. A small group slunk toward the Union guard as if to desert, a common occurrence by then.

Suddenly, the rebels rushed the guard and beat him over the head. Another Union picket ran, firing and yelling, "The rebels are coming!"[5] Ten thousand Southerners surged forward, led by small bands of sharpshooters. Most of the federal soldiers were asleep when the assault reached the first battery and were not able to resist.

Another contingent of rebel sharpshooters, under Joseph Carson, crept closer to Fort Stedman. At once, the fort's artillery ignited, and Carson's men sprinted under the guns' range. After navigating the spiked-log barricades, they entered the fort.

In the darkness, the Confederates captured three batteries, overran Fort Stedman, and gained 1,000 yards (914 m) of trenches. Yet as the sun rose, Yankee reinforcements marched up the hill, and Union artillery gained sight of their targets. With the help of the fort's guns, the infantry pushed the rebels back. It was the last offensive of the Army of Northern Virginia.

The Battle of Five Forks

One week later, the attack Lee dreaded came. Grant sent Sheridan and twelve thousand cavalry to a road junction called Five Forks to sever the last railroad into Petersburg. Lee's ragged cavalry held off Sheridan's first advance, but the next day, the reinforced federal army attacked from two angles.

On his horse, Sheridan led a charge over the dirt wall of the Confederate fortifications. Soon, the infantry had encircled the Southern army and captured five thousand Confederates. After another Union victory the next morning, Lee evacuated both Petersburg and Richmond. Sheridan pursued and forced Lee's army to turn west, toward Appomattox.

Forward to Richmond

When Lincoln heard the Confederate capital was in Union hands, he exclaimed, "Thank God that I have lived to see this! It seems to me that I have been dreaming a horrid dream for four years, and now the nightmare is gone. I want to see Richmond."[6] On April 4, 1865, Lincoln walked Richmond's streets. A crowd of black men, women, and children quickly surrounded him, shouting, laughing, and crying.

The day following the Southerners' evacuation of Richmond, Lincoln toured the city. Black residents flocked to the president to express their gratitude for emancipation.

Lincoln's emotions also soared, despite the hard stares of whites, as he moved into the city center.

Pursuit

On April 6, Sheridan attacked at Sailor's Creek. Sixteen thousand federals encircled eleven thousand tired and hungry Southerners hoping to reach supplies. The Union took thousands of prisoners, depriving Lee of one-fourth of his entire army. The next morning, Lincoln read a telegram from Sheridan to Grant. "If the thing be pressed, I think Lee will surrender." Lincoln wired Grant: "Let the *thing* be pressed."[7]

Other provisions awaited Lee's men at Appomattox Station, about 100 miles (161 km) west of Richmond. But before Lee could get there, Union major George Custer learned about the hoard of clothes, blankets, weapons, medical supplies, and—most needed by the rebels—food. On April 8, Custer's Second New York Cavalry captured the railroad station and the supplies and pursued the fleeing Southerners. After five hours, the Union had gained a strong position on the high ground west of the village of Appomattox Court House—right in Lee's path.

White Flags

At 7:50 a.m. on April 9, 1865, the Confederates swarmed forward. Initially, they pushed the Union back, but more federal troops arrived and formed a noose around the Southern forces. Realizing his exhausted army was vastly outnumbered, Lee sent out a white flag. At 1:30 p.m., Lee officially surrendered to Grant in a farmhouse.

In the parlor, Lee inquired about the surrender terms. Grant sat down at a small table and wrote, "'The troops shall march by Brigades and Detachments to a designated point, stock their Arms, deposit their flags, Sabres, Pistols, etc. and from thence march to their homes."[8] It was more than Lee had hoped for. Yet it was what Lincoln wished. "Let 'em up easy," he had said.[9]

As the news of Appomattox spread, some Confederates gave up command without further conflicts. In North Carolina, General Joseph Johnston ceded his entire division—over eighty-nine thousand men from the Carolinas, Georgia, and Florida—to Sherman. Sherman gave Johnston's army the same terms: lay down your arms and go home. By the end of April, the Department of Alabama, Mississippi, and East Louisiana had given up. Other generals took their time. The commander of the Trans-Mississippi Department did not surrender until May 26.

Meanwhile, Jefferson Davis and his cabinet fled by train. On the way, on May 5, fourteen officials dissolved the Confederate States of America. Five days later, Union troops captured Davis. He would spend the next two years imprisoned at Fortress Monroe.

Lincoln's Reconstruction Plans

For four years, Lincoln had pondered the best way to heal Southern hearts when the rebellion finally ceased. He had already begun reconciliation, of course. Under the Proclamation of Amnesty and Reconstruction, Louisiana, Arkansas, and Tennessee had established pro-Union governments. Now as the war concluded, the president focused wholly on mending the nation.

Despite resistance from Congress, Lincoln insisted that only gentleness would truly restore the Union. Retaliation and punishment would only perpetuate animosity and rend lasting divisions. The closing paragraph of his second inaugural address, given on March 4, 1865, eloquently promoted this approach:

(continued on the next page)

(continued from the previous page)

> "With malice toward none, with charity for all, with firmness in the right as God gives us to see the right, let us strive on to finish the work we are in, to bind up the nation's wounds, to care for him who shall have borne the battle and for his widow and his orphan, to do all which may achieve and cherish a just and lasting peace among ourselves and with all nations."[10]

In addition to amnesty, abolition made its way into Lincoln's nonnegotiable Reconstruction doctrines. The Emancipation Proclamation of 1863 had not included abolition for areas that had not seceded. Lincoln was deeply satisfied, however, when Louisiana included emancipation in its 1864 state constitution. Yet by January 1865, Congress had passed the Thirteenth Amendment, abolishing slavery throughout the nation. Now, the 1863 mandate that states embrace federal laws required the South to ratify the amendment to rejoin the nation.

After Lincoln's death, President Andrew Johnson carried out Lincoln's amnesty policy. Only Confederates convicted of killing Union soldiers outside of battle were executed. President Jefferson Davis, Vice President Alexander Stephens, Davis's cabinet, and state governors were arrested, but Johnson eventually pardoned them all. This approach drew angry criticism from Northerners who had lost husbands, sons, and brothers, but it earned gratitude and loyalty from Southerners.

Lincoln's Last Speech

Two days following Lee's surrender, an energetic crowd gathered outside the White House. The president's tall, lean frame appeared at a window, and he began a speech different from any he had given in the previous four years. This speech began with a cheerful greeting: "We meet this evening, not in sorrow, but in gladness of heart." Instead of rhapsodizing over the Confederacy's demise, Lincoln discussed the "great difficulty" of Reconstruction, or as he phrased it, getting the seceded states "into the proper practical relation" with the Union.[11]

As Lincoln closed the short address, he predicted he would soon "make some new announcement to the people of the South."[12] From the previous lines, his meaning was clear. "That means [n——] citizenship," John Wilkes Booth muttered. "Now, by God, I'll put him through. That is the last speech he will ever make."[13]

Three nights later, on April 14, 1865, Booth slipped into a box at Ford's Theatre and shot the president in the back of the head. Abraham Lincoln had seen the nation through its most trying time, but he would not be the leader to rebuild it.

CONCLUSION

More than any other president, Abraham Lincoln lived daily in the role of commander in chief. In addition to focusing on a president's typical purview of the political goals and policies of war, Lincoln attended to routine matters.

The young technology of the telegraph enabled the president's daily involvement. Lincoln was the first chief executive able to communicate in real time with officers and officials. Within minutes, he could learn thc army's position, the enemy's strength, and the tide of battle. He could also issue orders. In fact, Lincoln daily walked to the telegraph office in the War Department's old two-story brick building. While battles raged tens or thousands of miles away, he listened to the transmitter key's mechanical tap dance, then wrote his own messages for the operator to release on the wires.

Forced to Command

Yet Lincoln did not set out to be an ever-present commander. At the war's beginning, he repeatedly admitted to his

The US Military Telegraph Corps trained operators, strung wire, and transmitted millions of messages to and from battlefields. The telegraph was instrumental in Lincoln's hands-on management of the war.

military inexperience and ignorance and submitted to the opinions of the seasoned commanders around him. That tactic, however, did not obtain the result Lincoln desired, and he took charge.

The president worked as his own general in chief for half the war. With his resourcefulness, pragmatism, and perseverance, Lincoln prosecuted the Civil War without proper support from the military experts until he promoted Grant. The president made mistakes along the way, but he also showed a natural ability to assess a military situation and prescribe an effective approach.

Any Measure

Lincoln also showed shrewdness in policy matters. He deftly used every possible approach to defeat the South, including interfering with constitutional issues such as habeas corpus and slavery. Lincoln viewed any action that would support victory and reunion as a legitimate move. "As commander-in-chief of the army and navy, in time of war," he argued, "I have a right to take any measure which may best subdue the enemy … I conceive that I may in an emergency do things on military grounds that cannot be done constitutionally by Congress."[1] Indeed, Lincoln's unconventional tactics drew sharp criticism, and some are still debated by historians today. But for Lincoln, the plan was simple—save the Union, at any cost.

Lincoln's Precedent

When the Civil War began, the commander in chief's powers were hazy, obtusely mentioned by the constitution, and barely used by Lincoln's predecessors. Partly because of the unique nature of a civil war and partly because of the incompetence of his generals, Lincoln commanded daily. Lincoln used his role to issue military objectives, commission new technology, jail dissenters, forgive deserters, and free the slaves.

Abraham Lincoln sacrificed himself to the unbearable responsibilities of a wartime president for one conviction—the survival of the Union.

Lincoln began the war hesitantly, taking a full month to decide on a plan of action for Fort Sumter. Yet he grew into his military authority in a way that expanded the role of the president for every chief executive to come. Lincoln's first vice president, Hannibal Hamlin, described two Lincolns: "the one who came from Illinois, inexperienced in wielding great power" and "the conqueror of a gigantic civil war, the emancipator of slaves, master of the political situation, and savior of the nation."[2]

CHRONOLOGY

November 6, 1860

Abraham Lincoln is elected as the sixteenth president of the United States. He is the first president of the Republican Party, which opposes slavery's spread in the territories.

December 20, 1860

The South Carolina legislature votes to secede from the United States. Mississippi, Florida, Alabama, Georgia, Louisiana, and Texas follow in January and form the Confederate States of America on February 8.

March 4, 1861

Abraham Lincoln is inaugurated as president of the United States.

April 13, 1861

Major Robert Anderson surrenders Fort Sumter in Charleston Harbor after Southern forces shell the fort. Two days later, President Lincoln calls seventy-five thousand militiamen into service. In response, Virginia, Arkansas, North Carolina, and Tennessee secede and join the Confederacy.

April 19, 1861

President Lincoln signs an order to blockade all Southern ports.

July 21, 1861

The Battle of Bull Run destroys both sides' hopes that the war will be short.

March 9, 1862

The first battle between ironclad warships occurs at Hampton Roads, Virginia, between the CSS *Virginia* and the USS *Monitor*.

April 6–7, 1862

After a Confederate surprise attack, General Ulysses S. Grant secures a costly Union victory at the Battle of Shiloh, Tennessee. Grant's tenacity impresses Lincoln.

May 1, 1862

After Admiral David Farragut's fleet captures New Orleans, General Benjamin Butler takes control of the city.

May 10, 1862

Union forces capture Norfolk, Virginia, after a visit from Lincoln prompts naval action. In evacuating the city, the Confederates sink the *Virginia*.

May 31–June 1, 1862

Confederate general Joseph Johnston attacks McClellan's troops near Fair Oaks, Virginia, in the Battle of Seven Pines. The battle is a stalemate, but Johnston is wounded and is replaced by Robert E. Lee as commander of the Army of Northern Virginia.

August 30–31, 1862

Without the arrival of expected reinforcements from McClellan, John Pope is unable to withstand a Confederate attack in the Second Battle of Bull Run.

September 17, 1862

The Army of the Potomac blocks Lee's advance into Maryland at Antietam in the bloodiest day of the war. President Lincoln uses the weak victory to announce the Emancipation Proclamation.

September 24, 1862

Lincoln suspends the writ of habeas corpus throughout the nation.

December 13, 1862

In a bungled attack on the Confederate fortifications outside Fredericksburg, Virginia, Union forces under Ambrose Burnside suffer catastrophic losses.

January 1, 1863

The Emancipation Proclamation goes into effect, and the military begins actively recruiting black soldiers.

April 24, 1863

The Lincoln administration issues General Order 100, written by Francis Lieber. The edict validates emancipation and the suspension of habeas corpus based on military necessity.

July 1–3, 1863

General George Meade leads the Army of the Potomac to victory over Lee's army in the Battle of Gettysburg, ending Lee's second invasion of the North. Lincoln hopes Meade will follow the victory by destroying Lee's army and ending the war, but Meade does not pursue Lee.

July 4, 1863

After a two-month siege, Vicksburg, Mississippi, surrenders to Grant. After hearing about the city's fall, Port Hudson, Louisiana, surrenders to Nathaniel Banks on July 9. The Union now controls the entire Mississippi River.

July 30, 1863

Lincoln halts prisoner exchanges after the Confederacy refuses to exchange black soldiers following the Battle of Fort Wagner.

September 19–20, 1863

After capturing Chattanooga, Tennessee, Rosecrans's Army of the Cumberland is badly beaten by Braxton Bragg's troops in the Battle of Chickamauga. Rosecrans retreats to Chattanooga, and Bragg's forces surround the city.

November 19, 1863

Lincoln gives the Gettysburg Address at the dedication of the Soldiers' National Cemetery.

November 23–25, 1863

As the new commander of the Military Division of the Mississippi, General Ulysses S. Grant breaks the Confederate siege of Chattanooga, freeing Rosecrans and the Army of the Cumberland.

December 8, 1863

Lincoln announces the Proclamation of Amnesty and Reconstruction, known as the Ten Percent Plan. The plan offers amnesty and is the first step toward bringing Southern states back into the Union.

May 4–5, 1864

Two months after Lincoln promotes Grant to general in chief, the Overland Campaign in Virginia begins at the Battle of the Wilderness. The Army of the Potomac loses the battle, but Grant continues the invasion of Virginia.

June 1864

After a failed attack on the Confederate fortifications outside Petersburg, Virginia, Grant begins a siege of the city, which supplies Richmond.

July 11–12, 1864

Jubal Early leads a Confederate advance on Washington, DC, but withdraws after reinforcements arrive from the Army of the Potomac. Lincoln witnesses the action at Fort Stevens on the city's edge.

July 20, 1864

Confederate general John Bell Hood fails to repel Union troops advancing on Atlanta under William Tecumseh Sherman at the Battle of Peach Tree Creek. Hood tries again at the Battle of Atlanta then evacuates the city on September 1.

September 1864

General Philip Sheridan overpowers Confederate forces under Jubal Early and drives them out of the

Shenandoah Valley. Sheridan's troops destroy the valley to deprive the Confederate army of the food it provides.

November 8, 1864

Voters, especially Union soldiers, respond to the Republican pledge of "no peace without victory" and elect Abraham Lincoln to a second term in the presidency.

November 16, 1864

General Sherman's army begins the March to the Sea through Georgia. The army emerges a month later outside Savannah.

December 15–16, 1864

Union forces under George Thomas destroy the Army of the Tennessee under John Bell Hood. The Battle of Nashville ends the war in Tennessee.

February 17, 1865

Sherman's army captures Columbia, the capital of South Carolina, and Confederate forces evacuate Fort Sumter and Charleston.

March 25, 1865

General Lee orders an assault on Fort Stedman outside Petersburg. Confederates initially overpower the fort but are repulsed by the day's end. A week later, Lee evacuates Petersburg and Richmond.

April 4, 1865

Lincoln visits Richmond and is moved by the gratitude of the city's newly freed slaves.

April 9, 1865

In the Battle of Appomattox Court House, General Lee attempts to break through the Union line blocking his retreat. He is quickly surrounded and surrenders to General Grant.

April 14, 1865

John Wilkes Booth assassinates President Lincoln at Ford's Theatre. Booth murders the president because of Lincoln's support for emancipation and black citizenship.

CHAPTER NOTES

INTRODUCTION

1. "Oath of Office," *Heritage Guide to the Constitution,* http://www.heritage.org/constitution#!/articles/2/essays/85/oath-of-office.
2. Craig L. Symonds, *Lincoln and His Admirals: Abraham Lincoln, the US Navy, and the Civil War* (New York, NY: Oxford University Press, 2008) pp. 42.
3. Abraham Lincoln, "First Inaugural Address," Bartleby.com, http://www.bartleby.com/124/pres31.html.
4. Ibid.
5. Ibid.
6. Harold Holzer, ed., *Lincoln on War* (Chapel Hill, NC: Algonquin Books, 2011) pp. 9.
7. Symonds, *Lincoln and His Admirals, pp.* xiii.

CHAPTER 1: "AND THE WAR CAME"

1. Abraham Lincoln, "Second Inaugural Address," Avalon Project, Yale Law School, http://avalon.law.yale.edu/19th_century/lincoln2.asp.
2. James M. McPherson, *Tried by War: Abraham Lincoln as Commander in Chief* (New York, NY: Gale, 2008) pp. 20.
3. Geoffrey Ward with Ric Burns and Ken Burns, *The Civil War,* New York, NY: Vintage Books, 1994, pp. 38.
4. Abraham Lincoln, "July 4th Message to Congress," 1861, http://millercenter.org/president/speeches/speech-3508
5. Craig L. Symonds, *Lincoln and His Admirals: Abraham Lincoln, the US Navy, and the Civil War* (New York, NY: Oxford University Press, 2008) pp. 45.
6. McPherson, *Tried by War,* pp. 79.
7. Geoffrey Ward with Ric Burns and Ken Burns, *The Civil War* (New York, NY: Vintage Books, 1994) pp. 53.
8. Ibid, pp. 60.

CHAPTER 2: CONSTRUCTING A WAR MACHINE

1. Geoffrey Perret, *Lincoln's War: The Untold Story of America's Greatest President as Commander in Chief* (New York, NY: Random House, 2004) pp. 71.

2. Geoffrey Ward with Ric Burns and Ken Burns, *The Civil War* (New York, NY: Vintage Books, 1994), pp. 68.
3. James M. McPherson, *Tried by War: Abraham Lincoln as Commander in Chief* (New York, NY: Gale, 2008) pp. 42.
4. Ibid, pp. 116.

CHAPTER 3: LINCOLN AND THE NAVY

1. Geoffrey Ward with Ric Burns and Ken Burns, *The Civil War* (New York, NY: Vintage Books, 1994), pp. 92.
2. Ibid, pp. 92.
3. Olav Thulesius, "USS *Monitor*: A Cheesebox on a Raft," Civil War History Center, Civil War Trust, http://www.civilwar.org/battlefields/hampton-roads/hampton-roads-history/uss-monitor-a-cheesebox-on-a.html.
4. David Dixon Porter, *Incidents and Anecdotes of the Civil War* (New York, NY: D. Appleton and Co., 1885) pp. 64.
5. Craig L. Symonds, *Lincoln and His Admirals: Abraham Lincoln, the US Navy, and the Civil War* (New York, NY: Oxford University Press, 2008) pp. 116.
6. Ward et al., *The Civil War* pp. 175.
7. "David G. Farragut," Civil War History Center, Civil War Trust, http://www.civilwar.org/education/history.
8. "The Generals and Admirals: David Glasgow Farragut (1801–1870)," Mr. Lincoln's White House, Lehrman Institute, http://www.mrlincolnswhitehouse.org/residents-visitors/the-generals-and-admirals/generals-admirals-david-glasgow-farragut-1801-1870.
9. Symonds, *Lincoln and His Admirals*, pp. 152.
10. James M. McPherson, *Tried by War: Abraham Lincoln as Commander in Chief* (New York, NY: Gale, 2008), pp. 162.

CHAPTER 4: COMMANDING THE COMMANDERS

1. Craig L. Symonds, *Lincoln and His Admirals: Abraham Lincoln, the US Navy, and the Civil War* (New York, NY: Oxford University Press, 2008), pp. 97.

2. James M. McPherson, *Tried by War: Abraham Lincoln as Commander in Chief* (New York, NY: Gale, 2008), pp. 131.
3. Trevor Nevitt Dupuy, *The Military Life of Abraham Lincoln: Commander in Chief* (New York, NY: Franklin Watts, 1969), pp. 71.
4. McPherson, *Tried by War*, pp. 102.
5. "Abraham Lincoln to George B. McClellan, Wednesday, April 9, 1862," American Memory, http://memory.loc.gov/cgi-bin/query/r?ammem/mal:@field(DOCID+@lit(d1543100)).
6. McPherson, *Tried by War*, pp. 68.
7. "Cabinet and Vice Presidents: Edwin M. Stanton (1814–1869)," Mr. Lincoln's White House, Lehrman Institute, http://www.mrlincolnswhitehouse.org/residents-visitors/cabinet-vice-presidents/cabinet-vice-presidents-edwin-m-stanton-1814-1869.
8. "Cabinet and Vice Presidents," Mr. Lincoln's White House, Lehrman Institute.
9. Geoffrey Ward with Ric Burns and Ken Burns, *The Civil War* (New York, NY: Vintage Books, 1994), pp. 243.
10. McPherson, *Tried by War*, pp. 168.
11. Harold Holzer, ed., *Lincoln on War* (Chapel Hill, NC: Algonquin Books, 2011), pp. 138.
12. McPherson, *Tried by War*, pp. 208.
13. Ibid, pp. 210.
14. Ibid, pp. 199.
15. Geoffrey Perret, *Lincoln's War: The Untold Story of America's Greatest President as Commander in Chief* (New York, NY: Random House, 2004), pp. 212.
16. Ibid, pp. 211.

CHAPTER 5: NOT BY ARMS ALONE

1. Geoffrey Ward with Ric Burns and Ken Burns, *The Civil War* (New York, NY: Vintage Books, 1994), pp. 51.
2. Ibid, pp. 51.
3. Ibid, pp. 51.
4. Frances Lieber, "General Orders No. 100: The Lieber Code," Avalon Project, Yale Law School, http://avalon.law.yale.edu/19th_century/lieber.asp.
5. Ibid.

6. Ibid.
7. Geoffrey Perret, *Lincoln's War: The Untold Story of America's Greatest President as Commander in Chief* (New York, NY: Random House, 2004), pp. 139.
8. James M. McPherson, *Tried by War: Abraham Lincoln as Commander in Chief* (New York, NY: Gale, 2008), pp. 186.
9. Craig L. Symonds, *Lincoln and His Admirals: Abraham Lincoln, the US Navy, and the Civil War* (New York, NY: Oxford University Press, 2008), pp. 162.
10. Ibid, pp. 164.
11. Ward et al., *The Civil War*, pp. 125.
12. Perret, *Lincoln's War* pp. 202.
13. Symonds, *Lincoln and His Admirals*, pp. 178.
14. Ward et al., *The Civil War*. pp. 133.
15. Abraham Lincoln, "Emancipation Proclamation," Our Documents, https://www.ourdocuments.gov/doc.php?doc=34&page=transcript.
16. McPherson, *Tried by War*, pp. 192.
17. Ibid, pp. 192.
18. Perret, *Lincoln's War*, pp. 230.
19. Ward et al., *The Civil War*, pp. 170.
20. Lincoln, "Emancipation Proclamation."
21. McPherson, *Tried by War*, pp. 269.
22. Lincoln, "Emancipation Proclamation."
23. Ibid, pp. 280.

CHAPTER 6: PERSEVERANCE AND SACRIFICE

1. James M. McPherson, *Tried by War: Abraham Lincoln as Commander in Chief* (New York, NY: Gale, 2008), pp. 298.
2. Ibid, pp. 302.
3. Ibid, pp. 306.
4. Ibid, pp. 305.
5. Ibid, pp. 307.
6. Ibid, pp. 309.

7. Craig L. Symonds, *Lincoln and His Admirals: Abraham Lincoln, the US Navy, and the Civil War* (New York, NY: Oxford University Press, 2008), pp. 240; and McPherson, *Tried by War*, pp. 308.
8. Trevor Nevitt Dupuy, *The Military Life of Abraham Lincoln: Commander in Chief* (New York, NY: Franklin Watts, 1969), pp. 128.
9. Abraham Lincoln, "The Gettysburg Address," Abraham Lincoln Online, http://www.abrahamlincolnonline.org/lincoln/speeches/gettysburg.htm.
10. McPherson, *Tried by War*, pp. 339.
11. Ibid, pp. 344.
12. Ibid, 334.

CHAPTER 7: GRANT TAKES CHARGE

1. James M. McPherson, *Tried by War: Abraham Lincoln as Commander in Chief* (New York, NY: Gale, 2008), pp. 358.
2. Craig L. Symonds, *Lincoln and His Admirals: Abraham Lincoln, the US Navy, and the Civil War* (New York, NY: Oxford University Press, 2008), pp. 349.
3. McPherson, *Tried by War*, pp. 368.
4. Ibid, pp. 368.
5. Geoffrey Ward with Ric Burns and Ken Burns, *The Civil War* (New York, NY: Vintage Books, 1994), pp. 256.
6. McPherson, *Tried by War*, pp. 404.
7. Ibid, pp. 289.
8. Ibid, pp. 415.
9. Ibid, pp. 388.
10. Ibid, pp. 388.
11. Ibid, pp. 395.
12. Harold Holzer, ed., *Lincoln on War* (Chapel Hill, NC: Algonquin Books, 2011), pp. 208.
13. Ward et al., *The Civil War* pp. 289.
14. Ward et al., *The Civil War*, pp. 289.
15. Geoffrey Perret, *Lincoln's War: The Untold Story of America's Greatest President as Commander in Chief* (New York, NY: Random House, 2004), pp. 36.
16. Craig L. Symonds, *Lincoln and His Admirals: Abraham Lincoln, the US Navy, and the Civil War* (New York, NY: Oxford University Press, 2008), pp. 141.

17. "Mr. Lincoln's Office: Pardon's & Clemency," Mr. Lincoln's White House, Lehrman Institute, http://www.mrlincolnswhitehouse.org/the-white-house/upstairs-at-the-white-house/upstairs-white-house-mr-lincolns-office/mr-lincolns-office-pardons-clemency.

CHAPTER 8: "LET THE THING BE PRESSED"

1. James M. McPherson, *Tried by War: Abraham Lincoln as Commander in Chief* (New York, NY: Gale, 2008), pp. 359.
2. Ibid, pp. 371.
3. Ibid, pp. 423.
4. Harold Holzer, ed., *Lincoln on War* (Chapel Hill, NC: Algonquin Books, 2011), pp. 287.
5. Fred L. Ray, "America's Civil War: Pre-dawn Assault on Fort Stedman," Civil War History Center, Civil War Trust, http://www.civilwar.org/battlefields/petersburg/petersburg-history-articles/americas-civil-war-pre-dawn.html.
6. Craig L. Symonds, *Lincoln and His Admirals: Abraham Lincoln, the US Navy, and the Civil War* (New York, NY: Oxford University Press, 2008), pp. 263.
7. Geoffrey Perret, *Lincoln's War: The Untold Story of America's Greatest President as Commander in Chief* (New York, NY: Random House, 2004), pp. 403.
8. Ulysses S. Grant, "Articles of Agreement Relating to the Surrender of the Army of Northern Virginia," Our Documents, https://www.ourdocuments.gov/doc.php?flash=true&doc=39&page=transcript.
9. Holzer, *Lincoln on War*, pp. xxvi.
10. Abraham Lincoln, "Second Inaugural Address," Avalon Project, Yale Law School, http://avalon.law.yale.edu/19th_century/lincoln2.asp.
11. Abraham Lincoln, "Last Public Address," Abraham Lincoln Online, http://www.abrahamlincolnonline.org/lincoln/speeches/last.htm.
12. Ibid.
13. McPherson, *Tried by War: Abraham Lincoln as Commander in Chief* (New York, NY: Gale, 2008), pp. 437.

CONCLUSION

1. James M. McPherson, *Tried by War: Abraham Lincoln as Commander in Chief* (New York, NY: Gale, 2008), pp. 445.
2. Craig L. Symonds, *Lincoln and His Admirals: Abraham Lincoln, the US Navy, and the Civil War* (New York, NY: Oxford University Press, 2008), pp. 36.

GLOSSARY

amnesty A pardon given to a group by a government.

artillery Large weapons, such as cannons, that shoot missiles.

battery A group of artillery, often in a protected location.

blockade The closure of ports to sea trade.

casualties Soldiers lost in a battle, including those who are killed, injured, captured, or missing.

contraband Slaves who came under Union authority and were considered seized enemy property.

flotilla A group of small warships.

fortification A military construction, such as a trench, an earthen ridge, or a wall, built for protection.

habeas corpus The constitutional right of US citizens to receive a trial when arrested.

infantry Foot soldiers.

ironclad A warship with iron plating for protection.

militia An army of civilians that a state can call to action in an emergency.

morale The mental and emotional state of a person or group.

picket A military guard.

reconnaissance The act of gathering military intelligence.

Reconstruction The period of rebuilding the South following the Civil War.

siege The sealing off of a city or area by an army with the goal of capturing the location.

strategy The overall approach of fighting a war, including military, political, and economic actions.

telegraph A technology that sends messages over electric wires.

FURTHER READING

BOOKS

Cummings, Judy Dodge. *Civil War Leaders*. Mankato, MN: ABDO, 2016.

Ford, Carin T. *Lincoln's Gettysburg Address and the Battle of Gettysburg Through Primary Sources*. New York, NY: Enslow, 2013.

Kenney, Karen Latchana, and Catherine M. Andronik. *Abraham Lincoln's Presidency*. Minneapolis, MN: Lerner, 2016.

Seiple, Samantha. *Lincoln's Spymaster: Allan Pinkerton, America's First Private Eye*. New York, NY: Scholastic, 2015.

WEBSITES

CivilWar@Smithsonian

www.civilwar.si.edu/home.html

Browse by topic to view Civil War items from the Smithsonian Institution.

Civil War History Center

www.civilwar.org/education/history

The Civil War History Center of the Civil War Trust includes battle summaries and statistics, biographies, animated maps, and videos.

Mr. Lincoln's White House

www.mrlincolnswhitehouse.org

The Lehrman Institute has compiled information and images about Lincoln's life in Washington, his policies, and his colleagues.

FILMS

The Civil War. Directed by Ken Burns. PBS, 2011.

Lincoln @ Gettysburg. Directed by William Kerr and Peter Schnall. PBS, 2014.

INDEX